The Return

Odara's Rise

CARLA J. LAWSON

The Return: Odara's Rise

Carla J. Lawson

**© 2020
3rd Edition**

All rights reserved. No portion of this book may be reproduced, photocopied, stored, or transmitted in any form except by prior approval of the author or the publisher, except as permitted by U.S. copyright law.

Published by www.diverseskillscenter.com

Developmental Editing by Fran Briggs

Printed in the United States of America

**U.S. Copyright 1-7972400118
ISBN: 978-1-7347924-2-3**

Table of Contents

Dedication 4
Acknowledgements 5
Introduction 7

Chapter 1: The Return 9
Chapter 2: The Garden 17
Chapter 3: Odara 23
Chapter 4: A Call for Help 31
Chapter 5: Alone or Lonely? 41
Chapter 6: The Visitor 45
Chapter 7: The Scared Council 86
Chapter 8: Sudan's Portrait 95
Chapter 9: Preparation 111
Chapter 10: The Battle 127
Chapter 11: Healing 145
Chapter 12: Reassigned 157
Connections 176

Dedication

This book is dedicated to my son, Andrew Lawson-Freightman. The love I have for you cannot be contained by the vastness of the universe. I want you to follow your dreams, believe in yourself, and never think that it is too late to do anything. I want you to look back one day at a time when you were 15 and I was 50. I want you to remember that I said I was going to write books and I did it. I want you to always see a bigger picture and then paint yourself into it. You are the love of my life and because you look at me with wonder, joy, excitement and love in your eyes, I am endlessly inspired to do more and reach higher. May the love I have for you keep the light in your eyes afire when the world tries to extinguish it.

Acknowledgements

There are too many names to include everyone who has supported me on this journey. The donations, phone calls, text messages, emails, prayers and social media sharing has been incredible. Thank you to every person who was a part of this process in any way. For the support I received from my mother Jennifer Blackman, whose love and understanding has no boundaries by space or time, I am eternally grateful, and I couldn't and probably wouldn't have done it without you by my side. For the time my wife Greta and son Andrew had to cook, clean and maneuver through life without a word from me because I was on another planet writing this book, I am in awe of your support and acceptance of me and my pursuit of a dream that literally surfaced overnight.

Lastly but most definitely not the least of all, my publicist Fran Briggs and Cynthia Johnson my publisher at www.diverseskillscenter.com.

Your encouragement, faith, advice, excitement and professionalism were the catalyst for me to present something to the world fearlessly. May the next two books in the trilogy surpass everything you believed I was capable of. Thank you; my heart swells for you both.

Introduction

Mutora, Asir, and Roma stood in front of the Sacred Council awaiting instruction. They knew that what they would hear would be of great importance. Never before had the entire Council appeared to deliver instructions.

Whenever a new warrior from the spiritual realm was created, a specific element was the chosen source.

As the members of the Council explained what the warrior would be responsible for, it was revealed that the chosen element would be fire, and the body would be female. This warrior would be special.

The Council patiently waited for the cycle of the Universe that would be right for her creation. It was inherently understood that she would be allowed to choose the physical forms that she would utilize to carryout her earthly assignments.

It was also clear that she would be one of the

strongest ever to exist; she would be gifted in ways that others would not be. As such, she needed to be able to withstand the perennial trials of existing in human form.

Her spirit needed to be strong enough to overpower human emotion regardless of any situation. Mutora, Asir, and Roma were charged with instilling this spirit into its first physical residence.

They were given three days to prepare themselves and three days to bring her to life. She was formed by fire.

When the Council finished with their instructions, they ascended back to the spirit realm. They prepared to witness one of the greatest warriors to ever fight for the good of the universe be brought to life.

1

The Return

The women I'd met at the club could raise the roof anytime they wanted. They were tried and true party girls in full effect. They were also clueless about who I was, and I was fine with that. Although two of them knew me from another lifetime, neither of them seemed to be able to access divine recall. It mattered little. It was closing time and we were all leaving, anyway.

It was a night of laughter with lots of dancing, drinking and the best music and time I'd had in a long time with strangers. I just happened to walk into a lit spot and decided to stay and enjoy it. I ended up closing it out.

As we headed to the exit, the five of us were chatting about how great a time we'd had at the club when a male voice from behind us enticingly asked, "Y'all ain't staying for the after party?" The women giggled—but not as to offend—before responding, "Oh, no. We're good."

The response was followed by the laughter of several men. I continued to walk. I was exhausted and looked forward to going home. Suddenly, I noticed a warm sensation in my hands that quickly escalated to fiery hot. With that, I knew trouble was around the bend.

The intensity of heat in my hands continued to increase. It was time to prepare myself for the developing turbulence. A few seconds later, I heard the violent and ear-piercing screams from the souls of the two ladies who I knew from another place and time. They were in the club being overtaken by strength and force.

I heard heart-piercing screams that sent chills through me. I was frozen by natural fear but motivated by disgust. I heard every punch and slap as though I was standing right next to them. The women were being viciously attacked and didn't stand a chance against their assailants.

I hadn't had to access the portal that I needed for this madness in hundreds of years. I had walked past many things and turned away to let things just be—but this was too much!

I slowly returned to the club; I noticed a woman's mortified face near the exit. Although it was frozen with fear, her body and soul were willing to help and fight, hopeful to live through the experience.

Quietly, I motioned with my hand for the woman to follow me. Then I instructed her, "Do nothing until I say so."

Something in my tone must have given her a sense of courage. She asked no questions and paced her steps with mine. I walked slowly calling on the ancestral energy plane that would fuel my strength. I allowed myself to feel the fire that I was created from and knew that I would have to reveal myself.

As we turned the corner into the empty hallway, there were six men high fiving and laughing. One of them passed a bottle as he said, "After these shots, somebody get those bitches to the room."

The two women were semi-conscious, bleeding, and trying to muster the strength to crawl, stand or run. However, they were hurt badly and only able to cry knowing what was possibly about to happen to them.

Both women saw me first. One of them in her state of haze, called me by my true name after motioning to the other woman to be quiet. One of the men heard, and then glaring in my direction he said with a wry smile, "Two more for the party."

I moved.

Quickly and with precision, I drew a sphere in the air and with outstretched arms, I chanted in ancient tongue, "No motion, but let them see."

Upon hearing the chant, the men instantly froze in their tracks and were unable to move any limb in their bodies except for their eyes. I called the woman who followed me and told her to get the ladies out of there.

Without hesitation, she helped them to their feet and slowly moved them to safety outdoors. The men, still shocked by their sudden state of paralysis, and attempted to yell. Once again in ancient tongue I commanded, "Silence!"

I walked towards them all and told them who I was. Their eyes were dilated by fear, and their minds were confined by confusion. I considered ending every single one of them for their lustful violent behavior but I wanted to send a message.

It was clear to me that my work on this plane had begun and this was my first assignment. One by one, I approached each of the men. Their eyes pleaded for their lives. I pulled their pants and underwear down. Then I tied their shoestrings together so they could feel the shame of being exposed without permission, as well as the helplessness of not being able to flee.

My next move took restraint. After seeing two women almost beaten to a pulp, I wanted the men simply to expire where they stood; however, I knew that the call for expiration was one that held a karmic price and required a debt of balance.

So instead of draining their lives, I graced them one by one with a touch. A touch to one face, a touch to one palm, a touch to one thigh, a touch to one neck, a touch to one back and a touch to one eye. I circled them three times before stepping back.

Their eyes followed me—bewildered and afraid. I reproduced my sphere into the air and chanted, "Remember this and from now on you will defend and help because you have been charged with protection for violating sacred vessels. You will only release when help arrives and your screams will be mighty." Then, I walked away.

The silence was momentary as heavy-footed police were running down the hall towards the club lobby. When they reached me, they asked if I was okay. I replied, "Yes." Then I told them that the assailants were in the adjacent room.

As one of the officers prepared to enter the room, I spoke to the wind that graced my cheek from the open front doors of the building.

"Open them up; but spare them."

As I walked away, the screams of the men were released. The places where they had been touched were opened. The men began to bleed profusely. They cursed, apologized, and begged for forgiveness upon seeing the baffled officers.

After the call came over the EMT radios for more help from the police, the women I helped were being assisted into ambulances. The one who recognized me regained consciousness but had lost that recognition.

Having seen what she saw and being very much alert, the other woman began to ask me several questions. "Why did she call you that in there? What was that name? I thought your name was Odara?"

I touched her forehead, before whispering, "Forget." Then I slowly walked away.

Heading back to my home, I thanked the wind and the ancestors for their support and began preparing my mind for the messages that were sure to follow the night's events. Messages always appeared whenever I had an assignment.

Once again, right when I was about to try and live a normal, carefree, simple life; it had begun. Amused and annoyed at the same time, I walked into my home. After getting comfortable, I lit candles and incense and began preparing my body for the work that had to be done in my herb garden.

It was the place where the earth meets my spirit for moonlit conversations.

I had taken the time to turn my home into my personal sanctuary. It always welcomed me when I entered. Removing clothing with every step I took from the front door to the master bathroom, I felt the release of the pain and fear that I had witnessed.

With the water as hot as I could stand, I showered slowly, deeply inhaling the smell of frankincense and myrrh mixed with the lavender from my soap.

It was freeing and helping me to release the evening's events. I was trying not to be concerned for the woman who called me by my real name. It was critical that I not allow myself to get attached to anyone or anything—even if it was kindred from another time.

Unfortunately, emotional attachments were problematic. They could mean the difference between life or death, triumph or defeat.

As the images of the two women who were beaten so badly began to rinse down the drain in

Lavender scented suds, I struggled slightly with the moment I had been called by my name.

It was a whisper from someone who was almost incoherent due to the depth of her pain, but it was my name and for her to know it she would have had to remember it. Some part of her spirit had accessed a memory that recognized me from a time when I didn't have to acquiesce to society.

It was a time when I was able to show myself freely and was given full respect but not feared for who I was. That memory was during a time when people hadn't been overcome by the battle between good and evil, a time when there were no rich nor poor. There were only people co-existing peacefully. It was a time that was long gone.

Stepping out of the shower, I caught a glimpse of myself in the mirror. Pleased with the definition of my calves and arms, I realized I was still most comfortable when I was unclothed.

I was pleased to see that despite a strong love for pepperoni pizza and French fries, my body still had the silhouette of a warrior. I was strong and without the multitude of physical scars with which my spirit was covered.

I opened the curtains in the bedroom to welcome the moonlight. The moon was always one of my favorite sights. Sometimes I could actually feel moonlight bathing me with love and bidding and blessing me at the same time.

Glancing at the clock, I saw that I had about three hours before sunlight. I needed at least two of those in communion with the earth, so I quickly oiled my body in Sandalwood and patted myself down with powdered Hyssop from my garden. I slid into a pair of yoga pants and a tank top before grabbing my oil lamp.

Barefoot and humbled, I headed downstairs and out into my yard to tend to my garden and wait for the instructions for my newest assignment to reveal itself through the soil and roots of the herbs.

2

The Garden

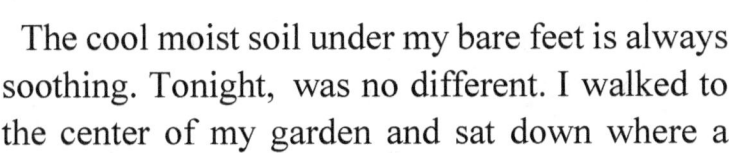

The cool moist soil under my bare feet is always soothing. Tonight, was no different. I walked to the center of my garden and sat down where a small altar and pillow were permanently stationed.

Looking around at the different sections, I was flooded with memories of what assignments had called for each of my herbs, sometimes combinations of them: *rosemary; lavender; feverfew; basil; apple blossom; chamomile; sandalwood; goldenseal; eucalyptus; belladonna; clover, frankincense; comfrey; buckeye, patchouli; purslane; sage; thyme; tobacco; valerian; mug wort; mandrake and hyssop.*

The herbs and plants were sectioned by purpose, protection and purification; cleansing and detox; prophecy and divination; love and attraction and sedation and defense.

My understanding of the full potential of their power was extensive.

The deities they represented were always given full respect. I inhaled the feminine power inside them when I worked amongst them addressing them humbly by name and with love. The memories were vibrant.

My first experience with any herbs was through a copper skinned, golden haired elder by named Aja three hundred years ago. She taught me the power of sacred space and how to cleanse it thoroughly with hyssop and sage. Aja was one of many elders who introduced me to the medicinal and protective properties of plants and herbs.

I smiled as I sat among blooms and vines in the fresh damp earth. The scent of lavender sweetly graced the air with peace and serenity. The moment was as amazing as it was brief.

As soon as I breathed in the scent of tranquility, my palms began to burn. I looked up at the moon and heard the sound of ancient drums. Immediately assuming the position of prayer on my knees, I closed my eyes and waited in silence for the instructions for my newest assignment. I definitely was not prepared for what was revealed.

While my eyes were closed, my garden came to life by arranging and rearranging itself to present a message to me. I could hear the rustling of leaves and vines as they maneuvered around me. I sat in silence, eyes closed, arms folded across my chest until all movements around me ceased completely.

When the garden settled, I looked up into the sky to give thanks for the opportunity to be used for the greater good again. I saw a lone bird flying, headed east. That meant my assignment would be carried out quickly.

Two rosebuds rested on the ground. A small pile of twigs lay atop uprooted valerian, and apple blossoms were scattered near a patch of comfrey. The rosebuds meant that children or young, reckless spirits would be involved.

The pile of twigs meant there would be a group of people closely connected and maybe even related in great danger. Those twigs atop the valerian meant that there was a deep love that needed to be protected.

The apple blossoms spread about the comfrey were what surprised me. They meant that I would be directly affected by an intimate connection and that there would be a need for healing as a direct result of it.

All in all, I understood that there was a family subject to some type of physical or spiritual attack and that the children were being used to cause the harm.

It was also clear that the well-being of this family was in jeopardy because they were just one generation away from changing fate to destiny. And something or someone did not want that ever to take place.

The love was in need of protection, but the intimate relationship involving myself and a possible heartbreak was puzzling. I hadn't allowed myself to feel or be connected in any way that could jeopardize my gifts or assignments for hundreds of years, so this part of my assignment to feel and heal was quite surprising.

I sat there as the Sun and the Moon began to exchange places with greetings of Adieu. I wondered, not only how it would happen, but also after so many years alone, with whom?

And it began like this....

3

Odara

I had chosen the name Odara for this lifetime. I liked the simplicity of it and the way it felt in my mouth. I was always amused when people asked for the meaning of it, or what it was short for.

It had no meaning that I was aware of, and I hadn't shortened it. I simply called myself into existence this time around and chose it "just because." Its only significance was that it was easy. I found out later that it was a Yoruba name for girls meaning Beauty.

I was okay with that.

I wanted this time around to have an easy simple life and just be. To travel the world, enjoy meeting people from everywhere, possibly fall in love and live a regular life having fun. It seemed to be heading that way for about forty-five years.

I believed that I could do it and expire this body without being called upon. My assignments

Usually came between the ages of twenty-two and thirty. I actually thought I had made it through. Apparently, this wasn't the case.

At forty-five, I'd been chosen again, and with a bit of wonder as to why someone younger hadn't been chosen instead, but I had no choice but to accept my path. Looking back, slowly the memories of being introduced to the spirit world and the physical world simultaneously began to formulate and swirl in my head. I sat still and with great reverence allowed myself to go back to the point in time and the place where I was given my first human form.

There were drums–lots of them. Loud and rhythmically, constant. I could feel hands, pushing, pulling, kneading and affirmations of power being spoken with every touch. The chants were melodic, almost song-like and I was very comfortable with the cool earth being my pallet.

As my body was being carefully configured, I could smell the heady aroma of White Sage and Frankincense, along with the musk of Myrrh in the night air.

Even though I couldn't see or touch anything yet, I was well aware that this call into existence was a full ritual. It was much different from the human birthing process I had witnessed so many times from the night sky through the eyes of others.

I lay patiently, hoping they would give me wings for whatever form I was to finally take. There was much emphasis put into the molding of my hands and arms. I wanted to see who was at work with my design, but I hadn't been given eyes yet.

The rustling of leaves and the sound of hurried footsteps was all around me. A male entity named Asir and a female spirit who was called Roma, were apparently in disagreement about my final arrangements.

An earthly woman named Mutora spoke softly but sternly about their disagreement. The arguing ceased. Asir moved what had become my arms and crossed them over my chest. While he was doing so, Roma whispered my name into my ear and placed her hands where my eyes and mouth would be.

"You will feel everything, you will see what others cannot, you will hear the voices of the earth, the wind and all who have proceeded you. Your journeys will be many; your body will constantly return. Your understanding will be supernatural, for you are a warrior for the greater good. Your weapons will be knowledge, timeless wisdom, gifts of the Earth and fire. We gift you with time travel, control of physical motion and the ability to heal and protect with the power of conjure.

You are born of purpose, light and divination. We bless you with the inability to be deceived. We seal your beginning with the depth and fortitude it requires to love unconditionally and use it to understand and accept all of humanity without it interfering with your purpose."

Then, there was silence.

I heard a scraping sound and Mutora's voice: "The fire you come from is the fire of love and majestic light. The moon will give you direction, the sun will guide you, the earth will provide for you wherever you are, and the stars will align themselves to aid you.

"The wind will speak. Fire will reside in you and must be respected. Water will move, and the ground will accommodate you. Be the greatest ever. You have been chosen."

With that, I began to feel the heat. The entire body that had just been created for me was aflame. What was probably a few minutes felt like an eternity as the flames covered me and then began to diminish on their own.

When the flames reduced to a smolder, my hands were outstretched and burning embers were placed in the palm of each one. Then the words, "Your call" were said aloud by Asir and Roma.

When the smoldering stopped, I was told to stand and see. I stood for the very first time and looked through my new, earthly eyes. What I saw was incredible. Spirits were in motion that welcomed me with waves and smiles. They swirled around me in flight and obvious celebration.

There were people on their knees and with their heads to the ground. They were in prayer position. Some weeping with joy, and others were giving thanks vocally in song. Looking up, the Moon cast a light over me, a welcome of love.

Asir spoke first. "Speak with clarity and definition. Always laugh from your heart and be discerning with your words, for they have wings."

Roma followed, "You are complete."

"I am your first earthly mother. No matter what body you reside in when you need me, you need only say my name," said Mutora. "I will appear in many forms but you will always recognize me, for I will always be female and I will always have a gift from this time in your beginning for you."

She then gave me a hug and said my name, "Machaneka." I wept from the fullness of the entire night's activities. With humbleness, I accepted the gifts I had been given and what I had been chosen to do.

Mutora wrapped me in a ceremonial robe and as we walked away towards what would be my first home, I looked back to see that Asir and Roma were gone, and the people who had been praying were walking away in the opposite direction. Magically, the spot where I had been created was covered in red, purple, yellow, white and pink flowers.

Without turning around Mutora said to me, "Never look back. What was once will not be again and anything that you need will live on in your heart and mind either as a memory or a map."

When in need, ask...

4

A Call for Help

The morning air came through the window fresh and crisp. A perfect breeze—cool but not cold—carried the blooming scent of fresh lavender and jasmine into my bedroom. I woke up with a smile in my heart.

I opened the doors to the balcony and sat quietly on a pillow in my pajamas thanking God for the beauty of a new day and whatever experiences it might bring. After prayer and thoughts of French toast and coffee, I showered and dressed while singing Earth Wind and Fire's, *Devotion.*

The day began with the powerful and lifting spirit of joy. I was going to maximize it by doing absolutely nothing. No work, no cleaning, no phone calls or pilgrimages to other planes. I looked forward to the opportunity to wander around the city and enjoy the sounds, smells, and sights.

My first stop would be the French bakery a few blocks from my home. It had the best and possibly only Chicory and beignets for the next one thousand miles.

I turned the corner onto the block where Café Printemps was located. The smell of fresh baked bread and freshly brewed coffee brought a smile to my face. This particular spot was one of my favorites. It had all the essential elements that I needed for a sensory overload of pleasure. There were always tables and benches outside no matter the weather.

The awning was a beautiful royal purple with gold embroidery. The tables were wrought iron with inlaid marble tops that were mosaic with gold leafing throughout. The chairs were also wrought iron with red velvet cushions and atop every table, vases of fresh orchids, dahlias and roses added to the ambiance.

Along with every place to sit having a spectacular view of the waterfront, tall green leaf plants and tall pillar candles adorned the patio. The interior décor of the café did not fall short of the outside.

Everything was perfectly placed for an inviting, cozy ambiance and the artwork of all the great renaissance masters of painting graced every wall. The perfect location, view and menu were a few footsteps away and I was delighted.

As I entered the café, I saw that my favorite window table was unoccupied. A young couple holding hands and a beautiful little girl sat a couple of tables away. At first glance, I saw the love in their eyes and the joy in their presence. But at second glance, I noticed that the little girl was staring at me quite intensely.

She was smiling.

Her ponytails and barrettes were perfectly placed. She twiddled a spoon in her little hands but she didn't take her eyes off of me. I smiled and said hello to them all and then I made direct eye contact with her.

"We're in trouble," came directly from her heart to my ears. I knew that she had no idea her innocent spirit was sending messages to mine, so I acknowledged her call for help silently with a return of, "I am here." Her mother responded,

Sudan stop staring; that's not polite."

I told her it was okay and that her daughter was beautiful.

"Every day for the last two weeks she has insisted on coming here for her cookies and milk. She's the joy of our lives and our only child so we come. Besides, it gets us out of the house for a walk and fresh air. It's almost like she's drawn to this place and she's definitely taken by you," said the girl's father.

I couldn't tell him that Sudan was drawn to this place because the spirit always knows what it needs, and children are the clearest vessels for spiritual communication.

I knew that she had been pulled to this place specifically to make a connection with me, and remembering my assignment recently received in the garden, I knew that this was the family that needed my help.

I wondered if the woman was pregnant or if they were trying to conceive. Once again I couldn't just blurt out. The thoughts were coming so fast and looking back at their beautiful baby girl, I knew that she was not the child in danger–it was another one whose entry into the world was critical.

Not to set off any weirdo alarms, I simply said, "Wow, someone loves quality sweets at a young age!"

Her parents laughed with me and agreed, and I walked to the counter to order my morning treat: Fresh beignets dusted with powdered sugar, a caramel sauce drizzle and a cup of fresh brewed chicory. The ultimate delight for me while on a physical plane.

I returned to my seat with deliciousness in hand and the little girl giggled. I made a couple of funny faces and winked at her while she swung her feet still giggling. Through the smiles and giggles, her eyes still unknowingly beckoned me for help.

I turned my attention to the conversation her parents were having and immediately picked up on some tension. They were discussing the option of trying to conceive again. Apparently, there was a risk involved with the young woman's health and the presence of stress in their immediate household due to a live-in relative was a point of concern and contention.

Sudan looked at her mother and asked when is Auntie Salisha leaving? Her mother took a deep breath, produced an obviously forced smile and replied, "She needs our help love; she may have to stay with us for a very long time."

Instantly, I felt the warmth in the palms of my hands–not the burning that comes with imminent danger but a definite heat that made my palms sweat. This woman, "Auntie Salisha" was a problem and a danger.

A big one.

I pretended to be oblivious to the conversation the young family was having and introduced myself. "My name is Odara. I am an artist and a holistic health practitioner."

"If you will allow me, I would love to paint a portrait of your beautiful baby girl! I will capture the joy in her eyes for a piece to go in my portfolio. It will take a few sittings of course, but you will be welcome to stay.

I will gift you with a giclee in the exact same size.

"Let me give you my information and business card so that you can Google my work and bio. I really hope that you will allow it. Sudan has a beautiful light."

The parents were thrilled, just as I knew they would be.

Who turns down any opportunity for the love of their lives to be captured forever for free? I thanked them for chatting, blew a kiss at Sudan and headed out of the Café.

Now, it was time to go home and wait for the parents to call and set an appointment for the first sitting as quickly as possible. It was the kind of sitting that would open the door to conversations. They would also be opportunities to build the trust necessary for me to help defend them against the attack that was looming in the spirit world with the child's mother's name on it. For now, I would just be patient, be still and wait.

When my thought's take over...

5

Alone or Lonely?

As I walked away from Café Printemps, I smiled. I was thinking about Sudan and her family. They radiated love. When her mother and father looked at one another, an obvious deep-rooted love and adoration for one another warmed my heart and gave me joy.

I was greatly moved to see love so innocently and overwhelmingly displayed. My mind wandered in love, yet my heart was slightly heavy. Despite always feeling so fresh whenever I witness true love, I am also reminded that I will probably never have that kind of love for myself.

The work that I was actually created to do did not allow for lifelong love commitments. It allowed me to love, but not to have a love of my own. That was part of the challenge for me. I'm subject to human emotions and experiences because I exist in human form. However, I must consciously separate from them because this body is just a costume. A shell, vessel or vehicle being used by the universe and the ultimate creator to help keep the balance between wrong and right, good and evil. It seemed so unfair.

If I had to be called into human form, I should be allowed to experience it all. When the bodies I inhabit are damaged or have aged as much as they can, I have the release of death. Why can't I have the joy of love, of building and sharing with someone? Perhaps even birthing a child?

It was as complicated as it was simple.

Having a family and raising children would be an amazing, exciting experience albeit a costly one. It would require soul ties, but soul ties would put all who I loved deeply in a constant state of danger.

The spirit world wars where I had dominated as a warrior for good could spill over into this physical plane. Consequently, anyone directly connected to me intimately might be subject to attacks from the enemies of good.

That was a price that I did not want to pay. To see others injured, killed, or futures destroyed because of the vengeful nature of a defeated bad spirit was not worth the pain. So, I chose to be alone. That means no husband, no children and no siblings.

An adopted mother or father figure was usually somewhere on my path. In this body, elders were necessary. So were a few friendships. I allowed them to grow so that I could have someone to talk to, but otherwise I had no actual family unit.

Occasionally, I could feel the emptiness of loneliness until I reminded myself that I was having a human experience, but it was quite minimal when aligned with my spiritual assignment. Purposefully, I now move ahead primarily solo. I am learning to be at peace with my destiny. After all, there is plenty of work to do that will require a lot of my time and energy.

The heart calls out...

6

The Visitor

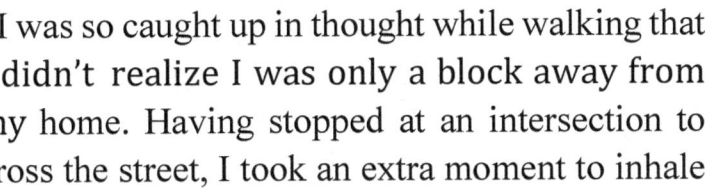

I was so caught up in thought while walking that I didn't realize I was only a block away from my home. Having stopped at an intersection to cross the street, I took an extra moment to inhale the fresh morning air and look around at the tree lined streets and homes ahead of me. It was always a beautiful sight and absolutely the perfect neighborhood for me.

Children still played safely outside. The neighbors always spoke to one another. There were family gatherings for holidays and special occasions that rendered the air filled with the sounds of great music and the smell of good food from all cultures. Just as I was about to step off the curb to cross the street, I heard the ruffle of feathers.

That wouldn't have had any significance any other time. I was in sync with the animals in the area. This was noticeably different.

This was the definite ruffling of feathers settling from a very big bird. Larger than anything that would be anywhere close to a residential neighborhood in the city.

Seeing nothing, I decided it was my imagination. Suddenly, I caught a whiff of a familiar scent of someone from long ago and very far away. It had been hundreds of years and thousands of miles away. It made me smile instantly.

The memory of what I had shared with that someone was intense. I turned and looked behind me into the eyes of the only being I had ever shared the feeling called love.

I almost fainted. His presence was overwhelming and intoxicating for my human form. At that very moment, time stood still. I wanted to leave my body and take flight with him. However, that was not a viable option. We stood silently, face to face, hearts pounding in full conversation. No words necessary.

I was in a state of euphoric frenzy. There was no doubt in my mind that he sensed that.

With the demeanor of a perfect gentleman, he stepped forward and gestured for my hand. I accepted it before we crossed the street together. It calmed me.

As we walked to my home, I wondered why he was here, where he had been, and if something was wrong.

Did he know I was just processing the loneliness of this life moments before he appeared? And when—*and how*—did he get wings?

My heart was beating rapidly as I entertained a million of my own thoughts. We walked in silence. When we reached the perimeter of my front yard, he took a deep breath and said, "I can smell the lavender in your garden."

I smiled as we continued to walk towards my front door. He stopped a few feet before I reached it. As I opened the door, I could feel him staring at me intently. He looked around, surveying the front yard, his surroundings, and me.

Then, he walked up to the porch and entered the foyer of my home.

This was a new environment for us. We had previously shared space in much more primitive times. Although we dwelled together in Spiritual harbors, we had never lived in a home that was designed by one of us for habitation in physical form fully as human beings.

I watched as he inhaled the scent of each room. He touched the walls, my blankets, and ran his hands over the wooden sculptures I'd created. His eyes were full of wonder and seemingly—amazement.

In my bedroom, he stood in front of one of my abstract paintings titled, "Life" and became completely still. I approached him and said, "It's called ..."

"Life."

He finished my sentence.

We smiled and joined hands in silence. I knew that he had advanced in great measure as a warrior in another realm. There really was no need for him to take a physical existence anymore. And I was still unsure of why he was here.

Looking at him made me feel like a woman. I was weakened by his presence.

He had flawless skin, a beautiful smile, and eyes that seem to see through his subjects. That—and his chiseled physique—made him painfully beautiful.

I was vulnerable and soft, and he knew it. He asked if we could go into my garden.

"How do you know I have one?" I asked.

He laughed and replied, "Because this could not be your home if there wasn't."

I offered him something to eat and then mentioned that the garden is most beautiful at sunrise and sunset. Sunset was approaching, and I wanted him to see the magic that happens when the sky is in transition.

He accepted the offer and chose wine as his beverage.

I invited him to take off his shoes and make himself comfortable because any home of mine was a place he should consider a home of his.

With a nod of acknowledgement, he began to settle on the sofa in my bedroom.

I headed into the kitchen and could feel his eyes following me. I opened and poured a homemade honey wine into my favorite wine goblets. They are my favorite because I hand-painted Egyptian kings and queens on them. I then returned down the hallway into my bedroom.

My bedroom was my personal masterpiece in this home.

I meticulously thought through how to accentuate every inch of space that would become my sanctuary. I wanted the place in which I would rest every night to be as beautiful as it was peaceful and comfortable.

I had removed the walls from the walk-in closets to create more open space.

I also didn't want anything store din my resting space, so the bedroom that was down the hall served as a closet and dressing room.

Entering my room, I saw whom I knew as Shaju.

He was seated comfortably on my purple, soft velvet sofa amongst a myriad of orange and beaded gold pillows and throws. He took my breath away. Shaju was now barefoot, free of the long-sleeved shirt he had worn earlier, and he had let down his loose, beautiful locks of hair that looked alive.

His arms exuded strength and power even when they were in a state of rest.

Shaju appeared to be quite relaxed. I was grateful for that even though that was pretty much the only temperament he ever seemed to display. That is if you dismiss the times he is in battle. When that happens, he is a raging storm.

I considered handing him the wine and making small talk but realized that wouldn't work because he knows me better than anyone.

Then, I thought to just ask all the questions immediately that I wanted answers to. That wouldn't work because after six-hundred years, it would be rude to start off that way.

While I was busy being a girl over-thinking what to say, he looked at me and laughed.

"Stop it," he chided. "You'd think after assuming physicality over and over again that you would have mastered not over-thinking. Relax, Love; I will share much with you during this visit. I'm here because I heard your heart cry out."

I responded, "You sent out a distress signal and I answered. I haven't assumed a body in quite some time. That's why it took me a minute to respond. My name here in this body is Jerod.

I heard you the first time when you answered the call for your current assignment. I believe that I told you before that wherever you were, I would always hear you. I'm hoping that one of those goblets holds a really great amount of honey wine and that you will remember who we were, who we are and stop being so human."

I handed him his wine and sat down on the floor in front of the sofa. I surrendered completely to this moment in time when I looked up at him.

"Hello Machaneka, you are here with me now aren't you?" he asked with a smile.

Hearing my real name and seeing him through my spiritual eyes opened something deep down inside of me.

I responded in ancient sacred tongue, "It is always a pleasure to be anywhere that you are. Welcome to my home. You have been missed. There is much I would like to share with you as well before you leave."

He exhaled and then smiled before we held up our goblets and toasted.

"Let's go out to the garden," I suggested. "I believe that you will appreciate the symphony that it provides at sunset."

Jerod followed me onto the balcony where we stood overlooking the garden from the top of the stairs. The wind blew gently. The wind chimes promptly responded by softly serenading us.

He waited patiently for me to take the lead. He knew that my garden was a sacred place and that it could only be entered by permission. He also knew that the first step into my garden must be mine.

The entire garden had been blessed and set up for the sole purpose of aiding me in my assignments.

That meant, if a stranger set foot into it without me leading, everything in it would retreat back into the earth until I bid it to grow again.

The plants, flowers, and herbs were designed for spiritual warfare. They could not be touched by humans without being released by me. They were not the everyday grocery store or nursery variety planted for viewing pleasure.

Nevertheless, they were a pleasure to behold simply because they were infused with spirit and life. The earth from which they sprang, was tilled and prepared with the dirt and water from sacred lands untouched by any natural human hands.

As the wind quietly circled us and the chimes began to diminish slightly, the Sun began her descent. I took Jerod's hand and led him down the stairs. We followed the stone path that circled the entire garden, slowly, as the Sun continued to disappear.

He followed me to the center where my altar, pillows, candles and a couple of plush throws were stationed. I motioned for him to sit and then told him to watch.

Jerod sat in lotus position sipping his wine and looking around. When I pointed to the apple blossoms, his eyes opened in amazement. The blossoms were opening and closing in unison. They were welcoming us.

He looked across the yard and saw the lavender plants rise and stand at full attention. Then, they began to sway with the same rhythm as the apple blossoms.

I pointed to where the mandrake was planted. He laughed aloud when the roots broke through the earth and began to dance side by side.

The Sage plants began to simultaneously emit clouds of heady aroma that floated and hung in the air. Jerod was speechless and smiling. He knew that he was receiving a gift.

We sat in gratitude and respect while watching my garden open up. It came to life in every corner and space it covered until the Sun set, completely.

We were so mesmerized and engrossed in the beauty and grace of it all, I didn't notice that we were in the dark.

The smell from the Sage, the sights of the garden, the symphony from the wind chimes and the Honey wine left me giddy. I turned to my altar and lit the candles that surrounded my seating area.

I picked up one of the throws so I could sit down again. Both of us were humbled by our surroundings.

I sat my goblet down and faced Jerod to ask him a question. Before I could open my mouth, he leaned forward, put my face in his hands and kissed me. I closed my eyes and surrendered to the deep passionate kiss.

My mind went blank, and my body yielded to his. It wasn't long before I realized we were in motion. Slowly rising above ground, he held me tightly, I curled up and then nestled into his arms and felt the soft down of feathers.

A set of wings wrapped around my entire body. They held me tightly, yet they were soft and comforting. I relaxed and rested my head on his chest and listened to what had to be several sets of wings still in motion. The ascent was magical. Time travel and levitation were not foreign to me, but actual flight was something I had never experienced.

In what felt like moments when Jerod gently placed me on a bed of leaves and moss, I was still in a semi-state of shock from the kiss and the journey, so I looked up at him and said nothing. He knew that I had a million questions and he waited patiently for me to take in my surroundings and speak.

We were now on a mountain top. The purity of the air filled my lungs rejuvenating me. The smell of fresh flowers, damp moss and frankincense spoke to my spirit.

Then I began to remember. Tears formed as the memories returned of Jerod and me as young spirits on assignment and of us learning what it meant to love someone in a physical body.

"Do you remember?" he asked.

I nodded affirmatively and smiled.

Looking up at him from where I was seated, I realized that he was not the young ambitious spirit that I once knew. His presence was majestic and emanated power and strength. His wings—now folded and barely discernable—were incredible.

Jerod's silhouette was amazing beyond words. I counted seven sets from what I could see in the dim light of the sky.

It confirmed that he had transcended to a level of warrior that I wasn't sure I wanted to attain. The respect I had for him was humbling.

When I lowered my head to sit near his feet, he said "Look at me. I have a lot to tell you and I chose to do it here because there is no time here. The best place to have a conversation that may take days is in a place where time does not exist. Therefore when we return to your home, you will only have missed a few minutes and the assignment that you have been handed will not be delayed."

I looked at Jerod waiting for him to begin. He smiled, took my hand and began where we had left off centuries ago– newly married.

Before one day was spent as a married couple, he was sent away on assignment. I was heartbroken, confused and angry both as a young spirit, and especially as a woman.

There were no words that could describe how I felt when he announced that he must go. That was six hundred earthly years ago, but it feels like yesterday.

The human forms that I took during his absence held a blurred memory of him, yet the spirit that lived in those bodies held an imprint of love that didn't weaken or waver. I had accepted however, that we may never unite again.

Fortunately, that was not the case. Jerod was here with me about to fill in the blanks that plagued and sometimes haunted me because I refused to let him go.

I had held on because I didn't know how to let him go and I didn't want to. So, he lived in my spirit with me and I always felt that he was near. The last thing he told me was that he would appear when I called for him.

I never called.

The thought of him not answering was worse than his leaving in the first place. It was a risk I chose not to take, it kept the memory of him safe and the integrity of what we had intact.

His absence was untainted by doubt or disappointment. Yet, his appearance at this point in my journey surprised me.

Apparently, I unknowingly sent for him. Was it the fear of loneliness or the impending danger from the assignment? In either case, I couldn't turn away from what sounded the alarms in my heart.

What I did know was that Jerod heard them and he showed up.

I needed to know what had happened, what assignment was so important that he was whisked away the day of his wedding, and what catapulted him so far into the upper spiritual realm as a warrior.

"The day that we were last together was the best physical experience I ever had. I had come to your village as a young prince named Shaju, soon to be King in search of a bride.

"My family and tribe encountered many villages in search of someone who would be the perfect future Queen, he explained.

"My standards were high, and some felt that they were unorthodox. I was unbothered by that. I knew that whomever I chose would need to be everything that I required because I might never have the opportunity again in human form to have the experience of love and family.

"As we continued to cover the countryside, I saw some of the most beautiful women I had ever seen. They were presented to me in the finest of fabrics and jewels, exquisite hair and ornamentation. The women were polite, well trained, and in proper decorum.

"It was evident that each had all been taught what their role would be should they be chosen. None of them, however, was right for me.

"My traveling companions were growing weary. They felt that at least three of the fifteen women that I had passed on were quite worthy and possibly perfect for me.

"I was determined not to settle for less than what I desired, so we continued forward. That is when we arrived at your village. The reception from the Chief and the elders of your village was phenomenal. We were warmly received in grand fashion and immediately offered a feast fit for a King. Also, there were individual lodging quarters for all of us.

"I was not interested in the pomp and circumstance. For some reason I knew that my bride—my Queen—was here in this village.

"So, I politely asked if the potential prospects for a bride were ready for me to meet them. Surprised, but not offended, the chief said something to a young woman seated nearby him.

"She bowed her head to me and disappeared. In what must have only been a matter of moments she returned and extended her arm in the direction that we should walk to follow her. We arrived at what was the center of the village.

"There was a line of about twenty-five, young beautiful women assembled with about fifty elders standing behind them. As I approached them, I was in awe of all the amazingly beautiful women. The women in this presentation put all of whom I had seen prior, to shame.

"They stood side by side and looked straight ahead as I approached them. When I did make eye contact, they immediately bowed their heads.

"When I reached the last one, I was quick to notice that she wore no tribal make up. Nor did she have on the traditional garb that emphasized the shape of her body.

"All I could see were her arms. They were well-developed. Her head was partially covered. She appeared to have quite a bit of hair concealed under her covering.

"The draped gown that she wore was orange and radiated in combination with the gold scarf on her head.

"Her presence spoke to me.

"Just as I was about to get closer to her, my counsel whispered, 'They put no effort into this one. Let's go back to the first in line.'

"I pulled away from him. I almost felt like I had no control. For some reason, I was drawn to her.

"Once I was directly in front of her, she did not turn around to present her entire body for approval. Instead, she maintained her proud position of standing straight and strong and looked directly into my eyes.

"Not once did she drop her gaze.

"I extended my hand for her to step forward amidst many gasps and deep breaths. It brought upon a shock and silence that suspended the moment in time. Her eyes stayed honed in on mine as she took my hand and stepped forward.

"I knew she was from the same spiritual realm as me. I just didn't know if she was aware of whom she was. So, I silently tested her.

"I whispered in her ear in the ancient tongue unknown to humans, that only spirit warriors can comprehend and speak, "What is your name?"

"She turned her head to face me completely and said quietly enough so that only I could hear her.

'Machaneka-born of fire, in this space I am called Folayan.'

"We stood face to face in silence as our spirits soared above then circled around us. We fell in love in front of five-hundred villagers who had no understanding about to why we were staring at each other.

"I could hear someone in the background whispering. A male voice communicated that the potential queen to be was prideful, not showing reverence, and was disrespectful in her constant gaze.

"My counsel began asking a litany of questions.

'What are you doing? You can't be serious?'

'Do you think she looks like she will not be subservient?'

'Where are her parents?'

'Why was she standing alone?'

I never took my eyes off her.

"We smiled through spirits and with laughter in our eyes, for we accepted one another. I had to be reminded that formalities and the 'proper' ceremonial actions were in order for this choosing process.

"For me, it mattered not because I had found what I was looking for. However, for the sake of human tradition, I turned to the Chief of her village and asked where her parents were.

"The chief made a sweeping gesture with his hand and the same young woman who had escorted us earlier, moved quickly in the opposite direction of the gathering. He asked if there was anyone else whose family should be summoned. Still in a locked gaze with who I knew was my new Queen, I replied, "No."

"The crowd responded with loud murmurs.

"The mothers of some of the young women could be heard crying and speaking disappointment.

'Surely you would like to have a second option should her family object to your proposal,' suggested the Chief.

"She is my only choice," I responded with absolute certainty.

"The chief raised his hand and gestured again with a sweeping motion. The line disassembled immediately. In the space where nearly one-hundred people stood, there was now only myself, the woman I chose to be my future Queen, my counsel, the chief of her village and the village Griot.

"The crowd began to stir and for the first time since laying eyes on her, I turned to see that they were looking at—about twenty members of Folayan's family were walking towards us. They were a strong but strange assortment of folk.

"Her parents led the entourage. They were followed by her grandparents, six of her aunts and uncles, and twelve youth. The members ranged from the lightest of skin to the darkest. They were tall, short, heavy set and slim.

"The family exuded strength, dignity, and high self-esteem. I was pleased.

"I approached her parents and then respectfully dropped to one knee.

"With your permission and blessing, I would like the hand of your daughter, Folayan in marriage."

Her mother smiled quietly as her father said, 'Stand please.'

"With that, we were breaking tradition. This caused the crowd to stir in discomfort.

'Folayan is not mine to give to you. She has always belonged to herself,' he explained. 'If you can understand that, you may have the chance at her hand; but the decision is hers. My blessing is offered upon her acceptance of you; not before it.'

"The Chief glared at him, and my counsel responded by moving forward to reprimand him, but I waved them off.

"I walked to present myself to her maternal and paternal grandmothers. Both were as dark as the night. Their skin was smooth, and their eyes were bright with the fire of life.

"One stared at Folayan, and the other stared at me. Side by side, they stood as an impenetrable unit.

"With your blessing, I would like the hand of your daughter Folayan in marriage. I will protect her during my life—and even through the afterlife. I will honor and cherish her and love her like no man has ever loved a woman."

The grandmother looked at me sternly and asked, 'Do you know who she is?'

"The question incited muffled laughter and whispers of questions amongst the villagers.

"However, I knew that she knew her beloved granddaughter was not of this place. Perhaps even the entire family knew and respected her as a gift from God.

"Yes Mother, I know who she is," I responded. 'Then why ask us, instead of her?' She asked.

"They both extended their hands to me and I took them.

"The elder women then walked me to where Folayan stood and said, 'The young man has a question for you.'

"Shock swept through the crowd. The utter disbelief of my counsel was followed by verbal chatter and outbursts.

"The Chief stepped forward and struck the ground twice with his staff. He then motioned for me to continue.

"Taking careful note of how regal and beautiful she was, I tried to control my spiritual excitement. I offered my hand to Folayan. As she accepted it, I stepped up as close to her as possible without kissing her.

"Staring into each other's eyes, we inhaled slowly and deeply, together. Then we leaned towards each other until our foreheads touched. We closed our eyes and spoke through spirits.

"After a few minutes, we opened our eyes. Everyone watched with wide-eyed anticipation.

I took a step back and we smiled at each other. I motioned for my counsel to come forth.

"Bring everything," I declared.

"He appeared to be puzzled. The look on his face inferred that he wanted to protest—or at the very least, ask questions. He was eventually able to discern by the sound of my voice that my mind was made up.

"My entourage included several horses and an ox carrying gifts for the bride's family. Folayan and I stood quietly, hand in hand. The crowd began to bustle once again with curiosity.

"They weren't sure that there was a confirmation of our union as neither Folayan nor I had spoken a word.

"The curiosity turned to excitement as my tribesmen and five young women approached with the animals bearing gifts.

"The first offering went to the chief of the village. It was a large fur pelt that was gently unrolled and placed on the ground before him. Then, a small trunk was placed on top of it.

"Alongside that, a long slim box was placed. My counsel then pointed to the oxen and said, "There are twenty of the finest there for you."

"The Chief nodded in gratitude and motioned for the trunk to be opened. It had three compartments. One was filled with gold coins, the second was filled with silver pieces, and the third held five strands of perfectly cut pearls.

"Amid the oohs and ahhs of the crowd, he reached for the long box and slowly opened it. His eyes appeared to get moist and his head bowed as he unfolded the soft fabrics that were covering the object and then he lifted a staff from its packaging.

"It was incredible.

"The finest woodcarver in the northern part of the country had carved the most elegant of dark wood into a work of art.

"Collectively, there were several tribes represented. All of the Gods were represented: The Sun, Moon, ocean, and the earth. Each had protective mask images strategically placed to tell the story of creation on this staff.

The Staff was inlaid with 24 Karat gold, Sapphires, Onyx, Tigers Eye and Abalone.

"The chief was moved beyond words and raised the staff up in the air for everyone to see. The crowd took breaths of wonder and amazement.

"The second offering was brought to the feet of the parents. A larger trunk and two boxes were placed in front of them. Folayan's mother opened a trunk to see hand dyed and hand-woven fabrics in an array of beautiful colors.

"She lifted them one by one and scanned them with her eyes. Her hands slowly moved across the fabrics as if to acknowledge the quality and the softness of them.

"As she got halfway through the trunk her father reached down to lift the contents, ceremonial robing fit for a king and a hand carved ivory walking stick.

"The smaller boxes were full of gold, cowrie shells, and intricately woven pieces of jewelry for both parents.

"They bowed in thanks for their gifts. They were unable to speak due to the splendor of what they had received.

"Last but not least, a large trunk was placed in front of Folayan. My counsel opened it for her to see its contents.

"There were rare bird feathers neatly tied in bundles, several gowns of the finest silks with detailed stitching, scarves in the most beautiful prints and waist beads made of gold, pearl, rubies and sapphires.

"A young woman brought a smaller box to Folayan and opened it. There were several heavily jeweled hair ornaments, neckpieces and earrings. She was to choose her favorite to wear as a sign of acceptance of the proposal.

"Folayan selected the simplest one. It was a chain that had one emerald pendant on it with the matching earrings. She then picked up a couple of feathers from one of the bundles for her hair.

"The young woman removed Folayan's scarf from her head and her hair sprang free like it had a life of its own.

"She put the feathers into her hair and turned to face me. Her presence was breathtaking.

"I found it difficult to look at her and breathe at the same time, but I maintained composure.

"My counsel approached her with the other five young women who had traveled with us and said, 'This is your court.'

I replied, "She will choose her own court and attendants."

My counsel became immediately incensed. 'You are breaking all tradition and disrespecting the ceremonial process.'

"I looked at Folayan and said, "In the next three sunsets you will have to choose your court—unless you already know who you would have by your side.

"They will need to be whom you trust the most, upon whom you will be able to depend in any circumstances and under all conditions.

"Your court will be required to commit to serving, aiding, and accompanying you.

Have you any idea who they would be?"

"Folayan turned to the crowd. They were still in shock at her being chosen at all. But they were also in disbelief at the freedom of choice that she was being offered.

"She stepped forward into the crowd and they parted so that she could move freely. As she moved about, she stopped when she drew near to a group of young women who were kneeling. They had assumed the position of prayer and had not broken it from the moment the soon to be king had arrived.

"Folayan then bid them to rise. She acknowledged the crowd, and then looked directly into my eyes.

'These women have been my friends for as long as I can remember. They are my choice for my court. One of them has two children that must join us as well.'

"So be it," I responded. Then I nodded to my counsel and he walked over to the Chief and faced the villagers to speak.

'A future queen has been chosen from your village for our future king. We will consider all villagers of this place family from here on out.

There will be a ceremonial feast when the sun rests tomorrow. We will celebrate the matrimonial union and the joining of cultures as family.

The following morning, we will leave with the future Queen, and any of her family members that wish to join us and her court to travel to what will soon be the kingdom she will reside in forever.'

"At this point, we were supposed to separate while her family prepared her for the ceremony and travel while I prepared for the ceremony and the return travel.

"Much to the chagrin of my counsel, I chose once again to break tradition and protocol.

"Have my lodging space prepared for us. When we return from our walk, we will rest there together tonight."

"One grandmother approached us and pointed out, "All you have is now." She then turned and walked away.

"We didn't know what she meant, and we didn't dare ask. What we did know was that between the two of us, there was an absolute understanding that we did not want to be apart for not even a second.

"We walked hand in hand until we reached a clearing that provided a place to sit comfortably. The two of us then sat underneath an enormous tree. It bid us well wishes in our silence by gracefully dropping leaves at our feet.

"With my arm around her, and her head on my shoulder, we sat until the Sun set completely. Then we rose in unison and began our walk back to the village.

"The night walk was much different from the one that led us to the clearing. Something big was happening in the spiritual realm that we both came from.

"There were whispers and spirit dancers swirling as we walked. Neither of us had ever experienced this in the presence of someone other than ourselves. And neither of us had ever seen such excitement from them.

"We reached the village and headed to the outer perimeter where my lodging had been prepared for us. When I reached for her hands, they were afire. Folayan saw the question in my eyes and said, 'That is my call.'

"We entered the lodging.

"The priest who blessed the bedding, anointed our foreheads with oil as he passed us on his way out. The attendant outside of the door drew all the curtains around the dwelling. We were completely alone by candlelight.

"Do you remember any of this Machaneka, then Folayan, now Odara?"

Jerod's question startled me.

I was so engrossed in the memories of that day and in his total recall of every moment that I had gone someplace else with him.

With tears streaming down my face, I told Jerod that I remembered. I remembered every breathtaking moment. I also recalled that once the curtains were drawn, we almost tore the clothing off one another.

That was followed by deep passionate kisses and fierce powerful lovemaking.

Through tears now falling more freely I told him that I remembered the sound of ancient drums and thought that I was dreaming.

To my dismay, I wasn't.

The drums got louder and louder. Shaju wrapped me tightly in his arms because only spirits would call our attention that way.

We felt the presence, and then looked up to see three members of the Sacred Council at our bedside. I thought that the burning in my hands earlier was a call for me.

It wasn't.

When I saw these particular members of the Council beside our bed, I knew that the call had been for him. My eyes pleaded with them not to need him and be here to bless or guide us. I begged for them not to send him away.

Isis spoke. "You have consummated Physically and spiritually; it's time for him to go. There's much to do before you meet again.

Be thankful for the experience of love so deeply on so many levels.

When Shaju leaves, you will be reassigned as well, to another time and place. You cannot stay in this form after he leaves because you have become one and the grief over his absence will consume you and interfere with the work you need to do. I say it shall be so."

Shaju wrapped me up closely and tighter when Shango spoke.

"You have been chosen, war is near, and it will last for centuries. Your presence is not optional. Prepare your mind to set her heart free."

Kali, the divine protector was the last to speak.

"This village and your loved ones will have stories that will become legend about a soon-to-be King who defied all traditions while choosing his future Queen.

The legend will say that the couple fell in love at first sight. The connection was deep enough that the Gods freed them of their obligation to rule a nation. As such, they disappeared after the consummation of their commitment into the night.

They aspired to travel the world together and share many experiences. Deeply in love as forever companions, they knew if they were to remain at peace, it must always be this way."

I yelled, 'No!' before I buried my face into his chest. I remember feeling the wetness of your tears and then you standing to your feet. I recall a final kiss and embrace and you saying, 'Whenever you send for me, I will come. Know that you will forever be my Queen and my love.'

"Then, you were all gone. In an instant, the one thing that I always said I wanted—a love of my own—was gone.

"I wouldn't see you again for many lifetimes—six-hundred years in total. I felt the wail of grief building in my gut, but before it could leave my mouth, there was darkness. Then silence.

"I knew I was being re-assigned. When I opened my eyes and looked around, I was in the city of Amsterdam. There I was surrounded by the hustle and bustle of working folk moving about. Even though the body I had assumed was older than the one that I had just left, it was strong, healthy and impeccably dressed.

"I wasn't quite sure what I was doing there, but a smoldering fire in my heart spoke to a loss that I couldn't replace. That is what I remember."

Shaju, now here as Jerod, kissed me passionately again. In doing so, we reconnected through the energy between us. I trembled. It felt so good that it hurt.

Trembling, I screamed at him. "Where were you?!"

He pulled me close to him, wrapped me up in his arms and began again. With a tormented look on his face, he looked into my eyes and slowly he began speaking as if the pain from our separation was fresh, new.

"I returned with Isis, Kali and Shango to the realm of the Sacred Council in a state of shock.

I was torn between what I was created to do and forfeiting everything to return to a physical body. I, as Shaju, wanted to find you; be with you; love you--even if only for one lifetime.

"The elders of the Council were the gate keepers. When they saw that I was distressed, they comforted me and shared wisdom that immediately changed my disposition.

"This helped me to ground myself and be at peace. They helped me to understand that if I abandoned my position, I would have you only for one physical human life. That's only if I was even able to find you.

"You had been reassigned upon my departure and our time would be limited and once our bodies expired there would be no more for us to ever experience together.

"Had I accepted what was happening, I would have the opportunity to always protect you, connect with you, and love you. That's because our commitment was consummated under the watch of three Council members and that connected us permanently.

"When you needed me, I would always be given grace; and I would be pardoned when I needed to get to you for all time."

7

The Sacred Council

Shaju was going to need a realignment. Very rarely did a spirit prefer to hold on to the human experience once it was clear what was in store for the spirit. In this case, he was definitely an exception.

His love for Odara had transcended realms and he was in a frenzied, chaotic state. This was not good. Shaju had been carefully chosen by the Sacred Council to be the head warrior for the battle that was quickly headed into fruition.

As a matter of fact, Shaju was even more special than that. Before the final retirement of several spirit warriors, there was a ceremony.

All relinquished something to be given to a future warrior who would be the backbone of the battle for the highest good to prevail in the universe. The chosen warrior for these was Shaju, who I now knew as Jerod.

During his creation, the gifts from the eternally resting spirit warriors were blessed and then planted in his spirit. He would spend about four centuries in his travels having human experiences before he would be called to the spirit realm for major warfare.

He would also be required to learn all that he could about being human because it was critical for him to understand the depth of what happens to physical entities when the spirit world is overrun with evil and negative forces.

During his travels, Shaju would learn much about "people". He was always fascinated with their obsessions over things that didn't matter.

He would be allowed to have parents once and witness the most heinous of human actions against one another as people.

Then he would be allowed to feel true, unbridled, unconditional love and acceptance—once. After that he would have to accept his charge, the one he was created to accept. Shaju did not have any idea that every moment of his existence had been prophetically presented thousands of years before he was to be.

The Sacred Council consisted of powerful deities from several different cultures around the world. They all held the ability to change the course of the world as we knew it when they worked together for the greater good of the universe.

To be a part of the Council, all members had to agree to assimilate the spirit warriors from their various cultures into one giant force. With each of them having their own gifts and strengths, that made them the most powerful in their own regions. Together with the warriors that chose to help keep order in the universe, they were an unstoppable force.

The Sacred Council:

1. Isis—Egyptian Goddess with magical powers greater than all other Egyptian Gods. She holds power over fate itself.
2. Shango—Yoruba God of Thunder, lightning and justice.

3. Oya—one of the most powerful Orishas—wife/sister of Shango—Goddess of the winds, lightning, violent storms, death and rebirth.
4. Kali—Hindu Goddess, destroyer of evil forces, and Goddess of time and change.
5. Amaterasu—Japanese Goddess of the Sun and universe.
6. The Holy Trinity—The Father, The Son (Jesus) and the Holy Spirit—the triune God of Christian faith and unconditional love.
7. And Bitol—Mayan sky God who participated in the last two attempts at creating humanity.

The deities and the spirit warriors pull together to help maintain the balance of good. They have been successful for longer than time has been recorded.

This particular upcoming battle was different from the typical universal fight between good and evil. The opposing forces of darkness and chaos had been grooming their own legions of warriors and destructive forces in an effort to wipe out an entire section of the universe.

Their goal was not only to destroy the Earth and a considerable part of the heavens but to converge on the ancestral realm with madness and chaos so that the prevalent peace of all who had any would be soured and manifest eventually into total destruction of all life.

Jerod took a deep breath and began describing his initial introduction to the entire Council. They were a quiet storm with little room for romanticism or conversation about things that did not involve the balance and scope of their purpose.

"Shaju was given in detail the way he was created, the prophecy that preceded his creation and the reason he was chosen to be a leading force in this great cosmic battle. With humbled tears, he said that he accepted his charge and his destiny as truth and necessary. Along with the acceptance, he would always have access to me with the blessing of the Council.

"I have been in constant warfare since I last saw you. I only assumed a physical presence once for an intervention after the designated time for me to experience human interactions had expired.

"Throughout the different battles in the spirit world that controlled the outcome of wars, natural disasters, and the energy in the universe, I began to realize the power with which I had been entrusted.

"It was not always easy but the armies of warrior spirits that I led were mighty and numerous. Their charge is to fight throughout all time—with or without a leader according to the orders of the Council.

"In the last battle, I fought side by side with the archangels Michael and Gabriel, Osiris and Loki, but we were caught off guard by our enemies' strength. They'd worked on building a stronger army in an effort to defeat us.

"Their attack was so intense that Oya and Isis themselves joined us to assure our victory. When the battle was over, I was gifted wings by Michael.

'For your journeys as you see fit,' he said.

"That was the last of the warfare until what we are preparing for now. I am not just here because your heart called for me.

Odara, I am also here because the assignment that you have received plays a significant role in the outcome of the next battle. Your success with your assignment pretty much seals the outcome of the next war being victorious for us.

"The life that you are preserving in just twenty-three earthly years will be the one that makes a global impact. It will change the overall perspective of the planet from weary to hopeful.

"The planetary acceptance of hope released into the universe will have an impact on the enemy that will be crippling. It will enable us to destroy this last force of darkness.

"I have been in the presence of the Council more than once when there was great disappointment. They don't understand the wars on earth and the condemnation. People judging one another behind who they worship.

"They believe by now that it should've been figured out that all of them together are one and there is only one goal: for people to love deeply, be kind, caring, sharing, empathetic, honest and to grow.

"Unfortunately, they spend too much time trying to prove others wrong instead of focusing on how to live right in the name of God.

"Oya and Isis both say that it hurts, and the Triune is disgusted. With that being said, please know that I am near and watching. The love that I have for you will not allow me to watch you to succumb to great harm nor injury. Listen to yourself and move swiftly. Time may not be on your side, but Kali is only a call away."

I heard Jerod clearly, hanging on to every word that he spoke. I understood that this assignment was big. I also understood without him saying so, that I would be moving into a higher level of service upon its completion.

I put my head in his chest and inhaled his scent while processing the magnitude of the purpose for his visit. Without another word shared, we were airborne again—this time to return to my garden.

I don't remember him leaving. I remember the beginning of the flight home and then I was in my garden at the altar awakening from a deep sleep.

Upon looking around, it was if no time had passed even though I knew that several hours, maybe even a day had passed. I reached for the goblet from which Jerod had drunk his wine and took a sip of the last drop. I heard him say, "I'm still here."

Then I gathered everything that belonged in the house and headed back indoors to prepare for my next move. I needed to follow up with Sudan's parents and get them excited and open enough to trust me with their child.

8

Sudan's Portrait

The next day was surreal. I almost questioned whether my experience had really happened until I heard the soft ruffle of feathers while making my coffee. I smiled and went to put on some clothes so that I could go into my studio to make and return business calls and work on a sculpture.

My studio was a converted greenhouse in my side yard. It was full of light, open space and had enough room for me to set up different work areas for each of my creative mediums.

Tapestries from all over the world hung on the walls amongst finished pieces of work. There were poufs, bean bags, pillows and large rugs in beautiful rich colors spread out in different areas. I could rest or relax in any area where I was working.

My sculptures were stationed on tall pedestals sporadically throughout the studio. At times, they seemed to be a protective sentry standing guard over my creative space.

Everything in my studio had a name and had been blessed. Sitting on a purple velvet pouf amongst gold and orange pillows, I set my coffee down on a teak hand carved coffee table that was one of my favorite furnishings.

I went into a meditational state thinking of Sudan and her family. I asked the morning breeze to open the third eye of her mother's spirit so that she would not be hesitant to call.

Even though my palms were still smoldering at the thought of Sudan, I knew that everything would turn out okay. I gave thanks during my meditational prayer and sat waiting.

It didn't take long. After about twenty minutes of stillness, I got up to put some time into an unfinished sculpture and my phone began to ring. It was Sudan's mother.

"Hello, my name is Jacquelyn. My husband and I were out with our daughter Sudan at Café Printemps and you gave us a card with the invitation for Sudan to get a free portrait.

I was wondering if you'd like to come to our home and talk further about what that would entail."

Excitedly, I accepted the invitation for a late lunch in the afternoon and wrote down the address. I thanked her profusely for the opportunity and relinquished the call.

Now I needed to get dressed, invoke some ancestral guidance and protection, and gather some herbs from my garden in case of any unexpected mishaps.

When I arrived at Sudan's home, her parents were outside on the porch having coffee. Sudan was swinging in a swing hanging from a powerful oak in their front yard.

I greeted Sudan and the oak as I walked up the walkway. Sudan squealed with delight when she saw who I was.

"The artist lady is here Mommy!"

Jacquelyn and her husband stood to welcome me.

"This is my husband Samuel, and of course you know who Sudan is. Come inside. I hope you like

Eritrean food; I've been taking cooking classes on foods of other cultures and today was the perfect time to share a few things that I've mastered."

I told her that I loved food of all kinds and couldn't wait to try them.

We walked into the house and I was instantly rocked by two things—sensory overload from the bright colors, beautiful patterns, and the arrangement of quite an eclectic family room; and my palms which instantly became afire. This time, the pain was stronger than before.

Every part of every room that I could see was exquisite. Art, accessories, candles, statues, and the furniture were all perfectly positioned.

Compounded with the beauty of the spaces was the smell of delicious food simmering, sandalwood and musk incense, and a heavy, deep-rooted feeling of love swirling in the atmosphere.

The human part of me wanted to love them and be a part of the community. The home felt like what I had imagined and dreamed of having for myself and it moved me almost to tears.

However, the protector that I am as a spirit was silently sending alarms off in my head. I was being reminded to avoid attachments. There was work to do and a possible battle. I didn't know what is at stake.

So, I complimented them on the beauty of their home and sat down at the dining table to join them for lunch.

As Jacquelyn was setting plates on the table, Samuel told Sudan to go tell Auntie Salisha that lunch was ready.

Again, my palms began to heat up.

Then, I felt something watching me. Glancing to my right was the most beautiful Golden Retriever that I had ever seen. He was staring at me as he intently sat as still as a statue.

"That's Solomon," said Samuel.

"He just showed up on our doorstep one day as a puppy and we couldn't turn him away. We tried to find out if there were any owners missing a

Retriever, but after a couple of months, there were no responses.

We accepted that he was a gift. He's a great companion and he's been fiercely protective of Sudan from the day we brought her home. They have their own language that she speaks to him in and he actually responds. Imagine that."

I didn't have to imagine it. Solomon was trying to send me a message as Samuel shared puppy tales with me.

Solomon was not of this place and he recognized me immediately. I acknowledged his concern with a hand sign, and he barked one time and lay down on the floor. Sudan's skipping footsteps to the table turned my attention from the dog to her.

As her mother was preparing plates, she and Samuel took turns inquiring about what would be necessary for me to paint Sudan.

I looked across the table at this beautiful baby girl with the most beautiful eyes. She was alive with joy and wonderment. I couldn't wait to help them, and I was looking forward to painting her portrait.

While admiring her, I thought I saw a slight movement behind her chair but there was nothing there. Then the burning began again, and I put my hands in my lap.

A tall, mocha-colored, slim woman entered the room. Solomon stood at attention and did not take his eyes off her. Jacquelyn introduced her. "This is my sister Salisha. She lives here with us."

I greeted her and felt the presence of what had to be something close to, if not pure evil. She smiled, sat down, and joined the conversation about my interest in painting Sudan.

I watched her closely as we talked. I noticed she wouldn't look directly at me.

When Jacquelyn sat down, we blessed the food and began to eat. It was incredible. She had prepared a variety of meat and vegetable dishes along with homemade Injera that was probably the best that I had ever had.

I complimented her on a great success for her meal. Then, Sudan asked, "Can you paint my friends in the picture? I want them in it."

Before answering, I picked up the discomfort of Salisha at the mention of Sudan's "friends." She seemed to be nervous, but it was fear that I was picking up on.

I attempted to zoom in on it, but Jacquelyn leaned closer to me and said, "Sudan has a group of imaginary friends that she says protect her. When we asked her from what, she just says she doesn't know.

"She also says they never sleep. They like her dolls and they are always with her. We humor her, but in truth, we know that Sudan is gifted and don't deny that she really may feel something or someone with her all the time.

"We were convinced when she lowered her head and started talking to my stomach and said her brother was in there. We hadn't told anyone that we had conceived, and I was only a couple of weeks pregnant at the time. It was really mind blowing.

"During the end of my first trimester I started to get a little baby bulge. She rubbed my tummy every day and walked away humming. Samuel's grandmother was a seer. Do you know what that is?"

Before I could answer she continued.

"His grandmother had the gift of sight and people would come from all over the country to seek advice from her and see if she could see things for them. We assumed that some of her gifts skipped a couple of generations and showed up in Sudan. I hope I'm not weirding you out or anything," Jaquelyn said.

"It's BS, and I beg to differ." Salisha concluded.

I looked at Salisha and caught her eyes. They shifted right in front of me from clear to cloudy to dark and back to clear.

Something was trying to keep me from seeing it, from knowing that it had taken residence inside of Jacquelyn's sister. What—or whoever it was also knew that I was here for more than a child's portrait.

I heard a low growl and looked over at Solomon. He was also watching her and not at all pleased with what he saw.

I sent him a message that we would talk later. After setting a date for the portrait, we decided that the best way for me to capture Sudan would be in her room at home.

Sudan was excited by this idea and preparing to leave, I thanked Jacquelyn and Samuel for the meal. Jacquelyn insisted that I take a look at Sudan's room before leaving. Sudan stood up an said "Follow me please, Ms. Artist Lady!"

I followed Sudan, and Solomon followed us to her room. Before entering she whispered aloud, "She's going to paint all of us while we play."

I was tickled by her innocence and still impressed with the gifts that she was yet to understand that she had. Sudan's bedroom was a bright, well lit, and full of dolls, pillows and stuffed animals. She also had super-girly bedroom furniture.

There were hot pink, turquoise, and orange colors everywhere. She walked over to a small bench by the window and let me know that this was her picture posing spot and wanted to know would everyone fit in the picture.

I stood in the spot where I would set up my easel and paints. She waited patiently, posed, and nodded her head to something while I pretended to be able to see her friends.

Then I walked over to her and put a finger on her forehead. "Sleep," I said. She was out, immediately leaning back on a huge ruffled pillow.

I stepped back from her and said quietly aloud in ancient tongue, "Reveal yourself."

Solomon stood by my side and watched as nine forms began to appear around Sudan.

When they were all present, there were nine angels in childlike form surrounding her. They looked at me and with wings raised formed a protective circle around her.

All of them looked directly at me and bowed their heads in acknowledgment.

Then they were gone from sight again.
Sudan was definitely *not* in harm's way. She was well protected by an entire flock of angels who apparently had been charged with her safety from birth.

Solomon looked up at me, tugged at my skirt hem with his teeth, and then took a few steps towards the room directly next door to Sudan's. I followed.

Listening and moving carefully, I could hear from downstairs what appeared to be a slightly heated conversation. "Hurry," Solomon pushed. So, I stepped into the room he stood in front of.

I almost choked upon entering. The age-old stench of demon was present in this room and it reeked and made my skin crawl with disgust.

Quickly surveying the room, there were four entities swirling and moving about. They were angry, chaotic, mischievous, and amused by my presence.

"You enter; we enter," they said repeatedly.

They flew from corner to corner of the room stopping briefly before changing directions, and then they did it again.

Solomon ran over to a drawer and nudged me again. Then he retreated to the doorway of the room to keep watch.

Still listening to the subdued sounds of an argument from downstairs, I opened the drawer.

There was a small clear box in the corner.

Inside of it, I saw a bundle of baby blue infant socks, a baby rattlesnake head, what appeared to be one of Jacquelyn's dreadlocks, and a patch of dead grass.

All of this was sitting atop of, almost floating in what looked like blood. I quickly closed the drawer and left the room.

Standing in the doorway of the hallway, I put a binding block on the doorway. Anything that wasn't already out of that room would not be able to leave that room in physical or spirit form. I could hear the hissing of the trapped entities inside. They were angrier now than before. I warned them that I wasn't finished with them and then I went back to Sudan's room to awaken her.

"Rise," I spoke into her ear.

She sat up and looked around her, and responded, "They will all fit with me, won't they? I promise I'll have them all nicely dressed."

I promised Sudan that they would all fit in the picture and began my descent downstairs with Solomon leading the way. Salisha glowered at me when I re-entered the dining room area. She almost bared teeth.

It knew that I had been in her room and caused a disruption. Staring back at her, I waited for her eyes to change again.

"Leave her be, and leave this house now," I commanded in a low voice. Salisha smiled at me as I heard from the spirit that I had spoken to.

"No!" it responded. Her eyes went dark, and then blank.

"So be it. Prepare for battle then. You are not welcome here," I said. Salisha stood still as in a trance.

Then she said, "It was nice meeting you. Have a good evening!"

Without responding to her, I walked over to Samuel and Jacquelyn. They were engrossed in a conversation about baby boy names. I thanked them for a wonderful evening.

With promises to return in two days to start the portrait, I left their home and headed back to mine. There was a lot of preparation to do before I returned. I sensed that the battle would not be in private.

We would probably engage fully in front of everyone, and that was dangerous for everyone, especially Jacquelyn.

Let's get to it...

9

Preparation

When I returned home, I wasted no time. I knew what I needed to do and wanted to be at my strongest when it was time to go back to Sudan's home.

After taking a long hot shower, I made some hot tea. Once fully relaxed, I went into the room that I had converted into a closet and unlocked the large cedar chest that was in the corner.

The trunk was made for me by a master craftsman who only made things from wood, metal or stone at the request of the Sacred Council. The chest was indestructible and had been created for the sole purpose of containing ceremonial robes, gifts from the ancestral realm for warfare, and protective wear for engagements with adverse forces.

When I first received it over a thousand years ago, it only held one robe and a staff. Now it was almost full of ornately covered robes, belts, jewelry and other artifacts created by humans who were specifically chosen to create for the Sacred Council.

It was infused by blessings and energies from the spirit world to assist me. Kneeling in front of it, I spoke one of the incantations that had to be used along with the key to open it. There were different incantations for different purposes and needs.

Without the right words, the incantation wouldn't work; and words without the key wouldn't, either.

I remembered the first time that I tried to open the chest and left out a few words from the incantation. The key just kept clicking in the lock, uselessly.

There was another time that I couldn't find the key and repeated the incantation over a hundred times to no avail.

I finally figured out to have a side panel of the chest reconfigured so that the key was a part of the design. It would only reveal itself for me to access after the incantation.

"Me, Us, we call on you Ultimate Mother/Father God for access to that which is needed to fulfill our purpose once again.

We ask for spiritual food in the form of strength, we seek guidance, we humbly request that you reveal what will be of assistance and accept that what you present is divinely presented with grace for the greatest of all good.

Wehallate, shohalik, tonatidis mishobetah, uncalitodia-nosephta. Yahseh."

After a moment, a light began to emanate from the right side of the trunk and the key rose from the design. But I wasn't sure that my request would be honored.

The trunk had one other special attribute besides needing a key and proper incantations to open. If the Sacred Council received a request for assistance and did not feel that I would require any, it would not respond to my efforts.

I had bid it open more than once and nothing happened. This was to ensure that I did not become dependent on the Council and to make sure that I understood that most of the time, I as a spirit warrior was already equipped with everything I needed to complete my assignment.

When it did open, whatever I had been assigned to do, might require the assistance of something blessed by someone older and stronger than me.

I removed the key and opened the lock. Lifting the lid carefully, I braced myself for whatever had risen to the top of its contents for me to utilize, making a thankful note to self. I never had to dig through its contents and try to figure out for myself what I might need since I never knew what exactly might take place during a battle.

The trunk would rearrange its contents on its own, bringing to the top in plain sight what the Council had decided I might need. Everything else would remain folded and bound so that I knew that it was not necessary nor to be disturbed for the current assignment.

Usually one or two items would be on top, but what I was seeing this time was enough for me to understand fully that the protection of this unborn child and the security of its family was far greater than anything that I thought I understood before now.

In the center of everything was an orb. With one touch from me, it would become a part of me until I released it. It would magnify in size and shape to contain whatever I bid it to.

There were two sachets. One held a finely ground glistening powder. This was a gift from Isis herself. Once airborne, the powder would bring divine light to any atmosphere allowing me to see the actions of my enemies a split second before they executed them.

It also gave me the power to see the true strength and power of opposing forces regardless of how small or menial they appeared to be. The second sachet was much larger in size than the first one.

Inside of it, was a roll of gauze that had been touched by Jesus Christ, the son from the Holy Trinity. I instinctively knew that this was to be used to wrap Jacquelyn's womb and protect her child throughout her pregnancy from any harm whether it be physical or spiritual.

There was a scroll tied with a silk ribbon. It was a gift from Oya. The incantation was to banish an entity from the physical realm and contain its ability to harm others for eternity.

A small box rested next to an alabaster jar. The box was shaking and turning repeatedly. Its content was a rare gift from Shango, the God of Thunder.

When I opened it, there was a small sphere that held the power of mighty storms and would be mine to use until this assignment was finished.

The alabaster jar was beautifully painted and inlaid with jewels and gold. It was full of Oil of Abramelin. This oil, when infused with the anointing of the Council, protected one from a physical, demonic attack.

The oil made from cinnamon, myrrh, and galangal and was quite powerful on its own, but when it had been anointed by the entire Sacred Council, it was impenetrable.

Lastly, I saw a white kimono with the universe embroidered in gold thread on it.

It was a gift from Amaterasu, Japanese Goddess of the Sun and Universe. It was to be worn as part of my attire when I returned to Sudan's home.

I was taken aback by what I was seeing. The fact that there was something from almost every one of the Sacred Council was slowly sinking in. As a warrior, I knew that certain things were bestowed upon a warrior according to rank.

The more I acquired in my trunk and the amount of what was made available to me had significance. A few of these items were new to me.

A long time had passed when I knew exactly what was in the trunk. It was because either I had paced it there, or the Council had silently gifted me.

The trunk needn't be open for the Council to add to it. They did so as they felt I was deserving.

They also did so when a warrior was in position for advancement. Humbly, I sat on the floor looking at what had been sent to me, and gave thanks for the assistance.

Accepting the responsibilities I had been given, the human side of me had a momentary sense of dread and fear. I dropped my head to shake it off and heard the soft ruffling of feathers, reminding me that Jerod was still present.

Grounding myself first, I then removed the items, closed the trunk and went into the kitchen because there was even more work to do yet.

In my kitchen I had a hidden pantry built behind the wall that the refrigerator stood in front of. It would be considered any herbalist or natural healer's heaven.

The best part was that it was temperature controlled and spacious. It had shelves and drawers full of powders, roots, bulbs and elixirs.

To the natural eye, it would look like someone was heavy into natural healing remedies. It was so much more than that.

In this pantry, I often spent hours preparing things at the small table in the center of it. Along with what I harvested in my own garden, there were roots and herbs only heard of through folklore in this pantry.

Also included were considerable amounts of things that grew from the earth that no one in this planetary realm would recognize.

To top it off, there was a numerable amount of exquisite plant leaves and dried fruits from other dimensions that could be very dangerous and even deadly if any curious human or devious spirit took hold of them.

Everything in this pantry had been hand-picked by the eldest and most superior of healers that served the Sacred Council.

I always knew when the healers were in my pantry adding something amazing before they greeted me with instructions and blessings because the aroma that followed them wherever they went was one that couldn't be contained by any earthly room nor could it be mistaken.

It was a heavenly smell that had the aroma of fresh earth mixed with musk and floral notes. Whenever I smelled that scent, I was elated. I knew that I was being gifted and that gift came with more power, education and another skill set.

Sometimes it was just a small root, sometimes it was a bundle of bulbs, and sometimes it was an entire shelf of things. Every time, the gift was fascinating.

What I needed from the pantry today were things that could be found in any nursery or upscale grocery store. But the strength of what was in the pantry would be a thousand times that of the regular garden variety.

I needed some things for Sudan. She was very special, spiritually gifted and I wanted to leave her with something to help her grow into her gifts.

I was saddened that the only person who would have full memory of everything that was about to happen was the unborn child and, of course, Solomon their dog and assigned protector.

Even so, Sudan would innately know that she was gifted and how to use what I had given her to help hone herself to do great work on the planet. I pulled a lavender velvet box lined with scripture and healing spells written in Sanskrit from a shelf and set it on the table.

Every time I placed a vessel on the table with intention for immediate usage that vessel would reveal to me what I needed to put inside of it. It would do so by the images hovering above it, smells emanating from it or it would simply keep placing itself next to what should go into it.

"For Sudan," I said.

Then I sat in the chair that graced the table and lit incense and waited. After about an hour, I began to doze off. Shortly, I heard the swirl of sound of a singing bowl from afar off.

I opened my eyes and saw the outline of a sitting girl with her chakras brightly shining. I said, "Thank you," quietly and went to work.

I placed seven small bowls on the table and spoke aloud, "Reveal yourself."

Items on the shelves in the pantry began to rearrange themselves. I stood completely still until everything stopped moving.

Then I surveyed each shelf where something had been pushed forward that had a chakral color enveloping it.

The contents of each bowl would be used to align and magnify Sudan's chakras.

The bowls would self-replenish as she used them throughout her youth and young adult life until she stepped into a higher level of consciousness about her purpose.

Filling each bowl one at a time, I worked quickly. The first bowl turned red when I picked it up. The items it would soon hold were for her Root Chakra.

I went to the shelf where both sage and ginger were side by side in a red light and filled it with equal portions of both separated by compartments.

When it was full, it began to seal itself. I walked over to the lavender box and placed it inside. The routine was the same for each additional bowl.

There was Sacral Chakra, orange bowl, calendula flowers and Hibiscus tea.

Solar Plexus Chakra, yellow bowl, rosemary and fennel root. Heart Chakra, green bowl,

Hawthorne berry tea, seeds for planting roses, jasmine and peonies. Throat Chakra, blue bowl, red cover blossom elixir and eucalyptus essential oil.

Third Eye Chakra, Indigo bowl, mint to be used to make tea or chopped to be put into food. Crown Chakra, violet bowl, lotus flower root, petals and lavender tea.

When the last bowl sealed itself and was placed in the box, I closed it and looked to see if the silhouette of the girl with chakras was still there. If she was, that would mean that there was something else that needed to go into the box.

She was no longer there, so I put my hands on each side of the box to seal it with fire. It would not open or be opened until Sudan needed it. She would be the only person who could open it and it would just appear to be a decorative box to anyone else who saw it.

The last thing I needed to do in the pantry was get a small bag of Horehound seeds together. Horehound from the spirit realm was almighty during any exorcism and I was certain that there would be one.

I bagged the seeds, picked up the box for Sudan and thanked the pantry for its assistance.

Now I needed to prepare my body and spirit. I had spent almost nine hours taking care of everything else. That meant I had about a day and a half before the battle took place. I would be fully charged and ready.

After securing the pantry with a binding chant, I went into my room to take off my clothes and put on a thin, yellow robe. I let my hair free from bobby pins and walked barefoot out onto the balcony that overlooked my garden.

I always felt freest when I was unclothed. The night air was warm with a light breeze. It felt wonderful. I took a deep breath and walked down the stairs into the garden.

Some of the blossoms swayed to welcome me. I walked over to my altar and lit several candles. With outstretched arms, I made my request.

"I have been called again. There is a possibility of great danger, so I beseech you for your protection in its highest form. I command this space to be a preparatory chamber for spiritual warfare."

Then I held my palms out facing forward and assigned the perimeters of my space until I created a full sphere.

"I give thanks for what has been entrusted to me and welcome the opportunity to be used again by something greater than myself for a purpose greater than mine. Immerse and bathe me now. I am fully present."

Then I sat down in the center of the sphere, closed my eyes and began to transition into a deep meditative state.

While doing so, the temperature inside of the sphere began to increase steadily and the smell of protective herbs began to surround me.

Within the next hour, the sphere reached a temperature equivalent to a sauna. My body was covered in droplets of sweat and the offerings from my sacred garden, sage, valerian, frankincense and myrrh amongst others had consumed the air inside the sphere.

I stretched out completely with the full moon above me and allowed myself to be covered and bathed, purified and prepared. A couple of hours later, it was close to midnight, and I felt myself reaching what some people identified as a state of Nirvana.

I would remain in this position in the sphere until it released me. When it did, I would literally be full of the fire that I was created from. The bathing process would transform me into full warrior mode, and no human emotion or actions would be able to distract me. I would be a force with which to be reckoned.

10

The Battle

When I awakened, it was almost a day and a half later. The cool breeze from the late morning air awakened me. The sphere and the garden had released me. I sat straight up feeling fully restored and ready to meet and fulfill my obligations.

Then I thanked the garden for what it had given me before going back inside my home.

Looking through eyes that now did not have a filter, my thoughts did not take me to a place of worry or fear. Ready to take care of business, I went into the kitchen and placed everything that I would need to take with me on the table.

Glancing at the clock, I saw that it was almost noon, so I went to shower so that I could get dressed and head to Sudan's home for what was supposed to be a sitting for her portrait.

Instead it would end up being a battle for life.

I felt stronger than ever before. The protective bath always provided me a sense of strength and assurance, but this was different.

I was different. I knew that something had shifted in my abilities for the better. I also knew that today would be a day that changed my path as a warrior. I was ready and here for it.

When I got out of the shower, I was headed to my dressing room to put on my dress and the kimono that Amaterasu had gifted me when the phone rang.

Instantly before even answering, my hands felt as if they were aflame. I didn't answer it. I knew that it was Jacquelyn calling to try and postpone for another day. I knew without a doubt as well that we didn't have another day to wait. Today was the day.

The temperature increasing in my palms let me know that I didn't have any more time. I threw on a jumpsuit forgetting that I was heading to grab the kimono. I swooped everything that I had prepared for today off the table and rushed to Sudan's home. When I arrived, Solomon was in the window.

"Hurry," he said. So, I did. I rang the doorbell and Sudan opened the door with a concerned look on her little face.

"Artist, lady! Mommy said you weren't coming today! Come in. Mommy doesn't feel well, and Daddy is acting weird."

I stepped in and felt the presence of something strong and ugly. The air was almost stifling, and the entire house was dead silent.

I followed Sudan into the family room that had been so full of love and joy just two days before. Jacquelyn was on the sofa and appeared to be in great pain. She was half coherent, holding her womb, and mumbling. Samuel was sitting in the recliner, but something was awry. He was lethargic and looked like he was in a trance.

"See," said Sudan.

"Where is Auntie Salisha?" I asked.

Sudan pointed upstairs and Solomon went to the stairwell and stood guard. I sent him a silent "Good boy," gave Sudan a hug and began to work. I stood in the center of the room, and in ancient tongue from the spirit realm, I spoke softly.

"Control this space so that it cannot be interrupted by outside forces. Suspend all faculties of this family that may cause them to interfere with this battle. Let them not see what they cannot comprehend nor understand. I call on the great Kali-Goddess of time and change to aid me in suspending time and motion.

"Let there be no memory of what is to take place here except for the divine recall that the unborn child will have to access when he is of age to fulfill his purpose."

Solomon was still poised at the foot of the stairwell, intently watching the closed bedroom door that belonged to Salisha.

I retrieved the Horehound seeds from their bag and began to scatter them in the corners of the room and just as I finished pouring them in a protective circle around Jacquelyn, Solomon began to bark.

Salisha had opened her door and was glowering into the family room from her upstairs view. She hurriedly ran down the stairs screaming, "What are you doing to my sister?"

When she entered the family room, the demon in her smelled the Horehound and decided enough was enough. Salisha took a deep breath and passed out on the floor.

What stood in front of me now was an ugly dark bulk of spirit and it was pissed the hell off.

I couldn't fight it in the form of Odara as a woman—just as it had shed Salisha's body for this battle, I would need to leave mine.

Simultaneously, I assumed spiritual warrior form and released the powder from Isis that turned into divine light.

The entity made the sound of a wounded animal and momentarily shrank in size.

During that moment, I quickly poured the Oil of Abremelin in a circle around my physical body to protect it from being inhabited by what I was fighting in case it tried to flee by using me against myself.

That moment was just enough time as the angry presence realized what had just happened and then it did something I wasn't prepared for. It split itself in two.

Now there was definite danger. I expected for the second entity to attack Salisha because it had no further use for her as a host. Instead the first one rocked me with a force that sent me whirling while the second one headed towards Sudan.

I returned a spirit fracturing blow to the first one and called out for Sudan's "friends" to protect her. "Reveal yourself and cover the child!"

Instantly, the second entity was blown backwards, Sudan's entire body was shielded by outstretched wings and joined hands. The Angels were chanting in unison. I couldn't see a hair on her head for their covering.

The Angels created an impenetrable barrier that the demon couldn't get within five feet of without being thrown back. The first entity was stronger, of course, and determined to win.

It hurled curses in ancient tongue that lacerated my spirit but didn't do great damage because of the protective bath that I had taken.

I decided to go for it.

It was strong but I believed that I was stronger.

I knew that if I defeated the first entity, the second one would dissolve because it was just an extension–not a separate entity. Before I could move again, I heard a loud crack. The second entity was beating my physical body with fierce brutality.

I knew that something was broken and that even in the strong physical shape that my body was in, it wouldn't be able to survive multiple strong blows to the head and torso. Now I realized why Amaterasu had sent the kimono. It served to protect my physical body while I was in spirit form.

I heard a familiar voice say, "Now, Machaneka!"

That was followed by the flutter of large wings. Jerod wrapped up my physical body completely within several sets of wings, yet the second entity was uselessly flailing at them trying to get through.

With no further hesitation, I flew at full force directly into the first entity and released the exploding sphere from Shango upon impact. The explosion rocked the entire home.

Pictures fell off the walls, glass shattered, and doors flew open. The wail from the entity did not lack in volume. It was the sound of a defeated warrior going down kicking and screaming. The disruption of the first entity's form collapsed the second one instantly. Before there could be any reconfiguring or possible regaining of form or power, I released the orb that Isis had sent, and on its own, it extracted the entity from the room and contained it.

Without haste, I started the incantation for expulsion that Oya had sent in the scroll.

"We, the spirit warrior sentries for the highest of all good, call for the expulsion of this entity from this realm to protect Jacquelyn's and Samuel's unborn child.

"Let the banishment be so that it may never return in any form to cause or aid in harm to anyone.

"Sohalesekamutakinesnowakaleaslokemehtacard i uskeshwayduroshono-Metah!"

The orb began to glow and spin and then it was gone. I had accomplished my task but I was far from done here completely. I still had to tend to a family and a heavily injured body.

When I looked over at where my body had been assaulted, Jerod revealed himself completely.

The look of concern on his face told me that my physical body was in a bad way. He hadn't released his wings so that I could see it.

"Finish here. I will take your body home and Mutora and I will tend to it until you arrive."

Without awaiting any response from me, Jerod and the body I had assumed and called Odara were gone.

First things first, though. The house was wrecked.

Solomon stood near me, tail wagging. I stroked his fur and said, "You are a great protector, and so shall you remain in this family as long as you desire."

Surveying the damage, I went to the front door so that I could see everything at once.

"Back as you were!"

There was rattling and clanging and banging and then the house settled. Everything looked as if it had just been perfectly cleaned and was company ready.

Turning to Sudan, I knelt at the feet of the Angels who were still in a protective circle around Sudan and thanked them. They raised their wings in full salute and then were gone. Now to release the family and explain what happened without scaring them into a panic.

"Awaken and be of open mind. Access your spirit center so that you will see me as Odara and understand what I say to you. Be freed of all spells, curses, pain or injury caused before I arrived today. Understand that you will have no memory of what I share after I leave, but you will have an imprint for deeper consciousness and awareness. Release now!"

Jacquelyn sat straight up and looked at me with a puzzled look on her face. She saw the figure of Odara, but something was different. Upon sight, Samuel moved from the recliner to the sofa next to his wife.

Salisha and Sudan took each other's hands and then sat next to Jacquelyn and Samuel. Solomon walked over and sat at attention by Sudan's feet.

"Hello beautiful loved ones. I am certain that my appearance may seem a bit strange to you or that something looks different from the last time I saw you.

"I am using the image of Odara to speak with you and it is not really tangible. I am a spirit warrior from the realm of the universe that you may call Heaven. I was assigned to protect the unborn child that Jacquelyn carries inside of her from harm."

Jacquelyn took a deep breath and covered her womb with both hands. Salisha sat straight up and so did Samuel.

Sudan looked up and said "I knew you were special. Didn't I say it, Mommy?"

Jacquelyn with both eyes still on me said, "Yes you did, love. Lets listen to Ms. Odara, now."

"I will share what has transpired in your home today sparing a few details, but I want you to know before I start that there is no danger in your midst anymore and you will never be subject to it again."

I explained about our meeting and the first warning. Next, I explained the warnings I received while visiting and what I had found in Salisha's room. I told them about Sudan's "friends" who were really guardian angels who had assumed the form of children so that she would trust them.

I explained about the entity that had been using Salisha as a host so that it could cause Jacquelyn to miscarry. Then I described the battle and how it had ended.

Salisha had tears running down her face. She got on her knees in front of her sister and began apologizing profusely.

"I didn't know. I would never harm you," she repeatedly said between apologies.

Jacquelyn took her sister's hand and responded, "I know you didn't and it's okay now. God has truly blessed us today."

Samuel was holding his wife and looking at Sudan with a look of wonder. He was processing it all. Finally, he spoke.

"Sudan is from where you are, isn't, she?"

I smiled and told him not to worry. "She is all human but highly gifted. She will make you proud and do wonderful things throughout her life that will change people's lives as a direct result of her gifts, and you will be alive and well-able to appreciate, admire and love her for a very long time."

Jacquelyn exhaled and then asked, "What about my baby? Who is he?"

I responded as truthfully as I could.

"All I know is that he will be the catalyst for an entire planet to have the powerful gift of hope again and it will affect the entire universe for the greater good."

Jacquelyn looked at me and began to softly weep. I told them that it was time for me to leave because I had to attend to the actual body that they had met named Odara, but that before I was to leave, I had gifts for them.

I handed Sudan the lavender velvet box.

"In this box is everything that you will need to strengthen yourself and stay in tune with the universe.

"You needn't open it until it calls for you to do so, and when you do, it will be at your disposal and self-replenishing the contents in it until you are fully prepared to move into the second phase of your life as a young woman.

"Remember that the only voice that matters comes from you. Seek not others for affirmation or acceptance. You will be well received wherever you are and need nothing more to do the work you are here to do."

I handed Jacquelyn the sachet with the gauze in it.

"Tonight, you will take a nice warm bath and when you finish, you will wrap your womb with this. After you do so, you will feel completely relaxed and comforted.

"When you awaken tomorrow, the gauze will not be visible, but it will still be there and protecting your unborn child and you from any complications or interference with your pregnancy.

"It has been blessed by the Sacred Council of the heavens and infused with herbs that will make you stronger. For you Samuel, I give you the gift of sight."

I stepped forward and placed my right hand over his eyes.

"See everything. I speak this gift into existence here and now. You will be able to assist Sudan as she grows older and stronger. Know that there will be times when she will need to call upon you to use your gift.

Don't be afraid to embrace the gift of sight. It can be quite useful and helpful when respected."

I now stood in front of Salisha, the woman who I hadn't been sure if I would have to take her life to protect this family just a couple of days ago. She was still hurt and crying from the realization of all that she had done and could have done to her sister.

She looked up at me with tears flowing down her cheeks and said, "I do not deserve anything."

"On the contrary," I replied. "You were used and abused by something ugly and evil to bring harm to the people you love the most. You most certainly do deserve what I have for you. Lean forward and lower your head, please."

She did what I asked, still trembling with tears as I parted her hair down the middle. Then I sprinkled a small amount of the powdered light that Isis had given me on the top of her forehead where the part began to the nape of her neck where it ended.

"Never be deceived by the darkness again. With this anointing, anything that is not of good will not dare to use you again.

"I also gift you with the language of ancient tongues to be used for incantation purposes. You will be able to discern when other people have been hosted and will be able to free them from it with this gift. Look up at me, please."

The light from Isis's powder had already begun to penetrate her spirit. When Salisha looked up at me, her eyes were clear and bright from the divine gift of knowing.

I tore a small corner of the scroll gifted by Oya and placed it in her mouth. "Speak with purpose and only for good when the light has revealed someone to you."

Then I said, "Remember nothing, but use everything. I am leaving now. Meshalota!"

Pain is a mindset...

11

Healing

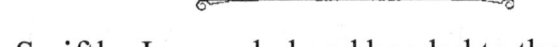

Swiftly, I ascended and headed to the place that I, as Odara, called home.

Entering the kitchen where there was an open portal, I wasn't surprised to see Mutora and Roma busy bustling about.

There were herbs and bulbs from my garden spread out on the countertop and they were boiling, mashing, mixing and pounding them all.

Without turning around Mutora said, "Assume yourself because your body is weak and needs help in regenerating. And open that pantry and grant us permission. We need stronger herbs."

I raised my hand and the refrigerator moved. Then I opened the pantry and stepped inside.

In my human form, I would have needed incantations and a ritual to get permission for someone else to have access, but in spirit form all I needed to do was command the room.

Arms outstretched, I spoke clearly, "Mutora and Roma will enter to gather what they need to heal both my physical and spiritual forms. Assemble for them and provide what they seek."

I took flight into the bedroom. When I saw my body, I was taken aback. Even though I was in spirit form, I had grown fond of who I was as Odara. The assault from the entity had caused much damage.

My breathing was shallow. Bruises covered my face and upper body, and my ribcage had been wrapped to support broken ribs.

The smell of blood was prevalent. Apparently, I had been hemorrhaging from an open wound as well. Then I realized Jerod was on his face in prayer position.

Without raising his head, he told me to take possession. I did so immediately.

The pain was excruciating. In human form, I was subject to feeling it. I was also subject to fear and worry. One of my eyes was swollen shut and there were stitches in my head. I couldn't move my upper body because of my broken ribs; and I had the distinct taste of dried blood in my mouth.

It occurred to me that the entity had almost killed me. Jerod gently placed his hand over mine and said, "Start from your crown and work on internal healing one area at a time. Your spirit took some lacerations, but it's still extremely strong and capable of saving this body."

Mutora and Roma entered the room and Roma who had opened my eyes for the first time when I was being created now closed the one that was open.

"Do as Jerod said while we tend to your body," directed Mutora.

They began applying salves and compresses to my wounds while chanting and speaking them into a healed state. I focused my mind on the contusions and busted blood vessels in my face and began to send light to each area. Slowly, one by one, they began to heal and disappear.

By the time I got to my chest area to address my lungs, Mutora and Roma were removing the wrapping that had immobilized movement in my ribcage area. Tears fell freely, from the pain, out of my closed eyes, but I continued to speak to my body and fill it with healing light.

A hot poultice was applied to my ribs and I began focusing on them while Mutora and Roma worked. For the next eight hours, as I worked on each part of myself internally, Mutora and Roma worked on my external injuries.

The pain was declining rapidly as we worked together. It took me a couple of hours alone to heal the broken ribs. When everyone stopped moving around me, Roma touched me again. This time she touched both eyes and said, "See now."

I opened my eyes and could see that I wasn't swollen. As a matter of fact, except for a slight soreness in my jaw I knew that we had saved my body and had near fully restored it.

Mutora took my hand and said, "A gift from home as promised for each visit."

She placed an amethyst amulet in my hand and added, "For your promotion. It's charged with restorative properties."

Then Roma smiled at me saying, "We are proud."

With that, they were gone. I was afraid to turn my head thinking Jerod was gone, too. Shortly after, he entered the bedroom with a tray of food and hot chamomile tea.

"You should be famished. Eat and rest. Tomorrow the Council will send a messenger to you." I sat up and smiled when I saw that he had prepared all my favorite foods to perfection.

"You cooked this?" I asked inquisitively. "How did you know what I like—no—love to eat?"

He laughed and said, "I asked Mutora what to prepare and she laughed and said, 'I'll prepare it; you present it.' I guess she knew that I have never had to cook anything ever."

Jerod sat quietly in a chair next to the bed.

When I finished eating, he took the tray back into the kitchen. I expected him to leave, but once again I was wrong. He climbed onto the bed next to me and gently put my head on his shoulder.

"Sleep Machaneka, now Odara. Sleep and be filled with peace. You were incredible today, warrior; nothing short of incredible."

And then he kissed my forehead and I sank into a deep sleep within minutes.

The next morning, I was awakened by the aroma of fresh coffee. Jerod came into the bedroom and said, "Out of bed sleepyhead! Let's see how your body is doing."

I sat up and then turned myself slowly to stand. I waited for the pain from broken ribs to kick-in and was delightfully disappointed. Then I put my feet on the floor and stood up.

Nothing.

I had succeeded in repairing myself internally. Mutora and Roma had taken care of my external wounds. Now to the mirror to see how my face was healing.

I approached it slowly, remembering what I had seen when I first arrived home from the battle. Standing in front of the mirror, tears of gratitude began to fall.

I had no bruises, no scars where there had been cuts and no swelling. I gave thanks aloud and then I sat down and wept.

Jerod put his arms around me and let me cry. He knew that my physical body had been traumatized and thus a physical reaction was only normal. We both knew that while my human form was crying, my spirit was soaring.

I had not only completed my assignment, but I had been restored and I was about to get a visit from the messenger from the Sacred Council. We walked into the dining room after I got myself together and sat at the bistro table by the window in the corner.

Then, the two of us drank coffee in silence. I knew that he was leaving. "Stop it," Jerod said. "I am always near for you." I nodded my head accepting the truth for what it was.

I still loved him. I would always love him. I couldn't help it. "I love you, too, baby."

He stood up, kissed me like it was the first time and he was gone. I sat staring at the spot where he had been standing for a long time until the sound of the wind swiftly approaching snapped me out of my trance.

The messenger for the Sacred Council always tickled me when he appeared. He found earth to be an amusing place and was fascinated by the daily ins and outs of people who primarily were focused on their own lives and not on the quality of the collective whole.

He also enjoyed assuming a physical form so that he could get dressed up–no matter when he showed up and what time period it was. He was casket sharp—fully dressed in whatever was the current time period's finest. He loved that.

When he assumed a physical form to deliver messages on Earth, he always used the same name, Phillip. I wondered how he would be dressed this time and the doorbell rang. I laughed aloud while walking to open the door, vaguely remembering a conversation with him when he had questioned the necessity of doorbells.

He couldn't understand why people needed walls or doors. I opened the front door and he did not disappoint.

Standing in front of me was an ancient spirit who moved like the wind. It was suited in a tailored navy blue Armani suit, crisp white shirt, silver cufflinks, white pocket kerchief, brown Balenciaga shoes and Hermes shades.

He smiled and said, "I rang the doorbell!" We both laughed, and I moved aside so that he could enter.

I offered him coffee which he politely declined.

"I have several messages to deliver today with urgency. There is much going on in our realm. And I have to enter at least five different time periods and parts of the world. You are one of two in the same time period and city. That is a rare occurrence if I may say so."

I almost spit out my coffee. *There was another warrior here? In the same vicinity as myself?* How had we not crossed paths or been made aware of one another?

Phillip continued to ignore the questions that he knew I wanted to ask. He wasn't here to satisfy my curiosity; he had an assignment to fulfill.

"Your message, Machaneka."

He handed me a small red satin box and stepped back to allow me to open it. I knew what it was, but I wasn't prepared for the beauty of it. I knew from hearing the stories of other warriors that were higher in rank than me that this was my promotion.

"Open it, please. You know that I cannot leave until you have received, accepted, and responded."

Phillip was excited for me, but his personality was much too formal to show any emotion.

I took the lid off the box and a small swarm of swirling light and colors arose from it. What looked like a million tiny butterflies began to swarm around me forming a cocoon.

Then a woman's voice which I hadn't heard before addressed me.

"You have been fearless, consistent, loyal, obedient, strong and unwavering. You are now of the second sentry in the spirit realm.

Your assignments will require the usage of all your capabilities to their fullest from now on.

"This appointment to the second sentry is the last one before total spirit assumption. You have been skipped past the third sentry for the warfare you just survived. Be of our strongest and our best. You have been chosen and promoted."

The cocoon fell to the floor, the swirling stopped, and I looked at my hands. They had the actual imprint of the burning embers that were placed in my palms during my creation.

I looked at my arms. They were chiseled and strong.

It was then that I could feel the hair hanging past my shoulders. I had acquired almost a foot of hair. It was beautiful and springing from my head like a lion's mane of natural curls.

No longer was I wearing my robe. I wore a sleeveless purple gown that had a stand-up collar and fell to the floor. My left arm had a tattoo of an ancient symbol for fire on it and I was glowing.

Philip bowed to me and said, "You are most worthy, we are all proud of you. Prepare yourself for transition. You will receive a call for another assignment within seven days and it is quite far from this place and time."

"Salumetah!"

Philip, the butterflies—everything was gone in a split second. I was speechless but thrilled after being promoted without knowing I was even near the threshold for promotion.

I was getting reassigned as a part of the second sentry *and* I was going to be able to keep the form of Odara. If it wasn't so, there wouldn't be any physical changes to my body.

He said seven days before my next call and relocation. Damn! I had work to do and no time to think about it.

12

Reassigned

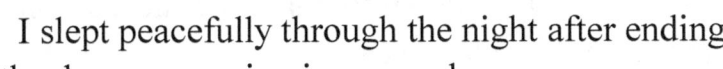

I slept peacefully through the night after ending the day communing in my garden.

The events of two days ago seemed light years away. I was giddy, excited, and filled with wonder. For the most part, I was ready for whatever came next.

After a brisk morning walk through my neighborhood, I returned home to begin the necessary preparations for my relocation. I wasn't curious about where I was going to be sent, but I did wonder who the other warrior was in this city.

I went into my garden first since it would take the most time to address.

I approached the first patch of herbs, my beautiful lavender.

"You have served me well here as the first to take root in this space. I bid you retreat now and take every living thing in this yard with you. I will call for your return when I have been reassigned and the first patch of soil has been prepared at my new home."

I then walked over to my altar, lit all the candles, and sat down to chant the incantations that would soften the earth:

"Protect the garden during its retreating process and then condense all of the sacred soil that has been used for planting into one small pouch that will be used when I was ready to recover the garden wherever I am reassigned."

There were several incantations that would take almost two hours to finish. I wanted to finish by noon so that I could rest, restore, and begin charging the items in my home that would follow me.

I then called on the Sacred Council to witness and support the retreat and transference of the garden. Then I began.

After three and a half hours, I was finished, and my body was physically drained. I went into the house to wrap up the pantry in a form similar to what I had just done in the garden.

Two hours later, I was still tired but unwilling to stop until I was finished.

I entered the sitting area that I had chosen for this space because it was the center of the house. Then I circled the room seven times and then touched the center of every corner in the room.

After releasing an orb into the air, I instructed it to charge. It moved through each room in the house freely, fully charging the ancient pieces of furniture and sacred artifacts to follow me.

The orb would show up wherever it was that I was to reside for my next assignment. Then, I went into my bedroom to take a nap.

What started as a nap turned into a deep sleep. I had depleted myself physically by using too much spiritual energy. I woke up to find that it was night.

I slipped into my pajamas and walked over to the bedroom window that faced the garden. Almost half of its growth had already retreated into the earth. Fresh grass grew where there was once a multitude of herbs planted in sections according to their purpose.

Pleased, I got in the bed and fell asleep. I woke up the next morning and decided to sit on my porch in the swing to meditate before having my morning Vanilla latte.

I was glad that I did.

While meditating, I thought about Sudan, who it felt like I'd met many years before even though only a few days had passed since I had met her and had a full-blown battle in her home. She was such a beautiful baby girl. I focused on her and then began to see her family in my mind.

They were sharing a meal, talking, laughing and arguing over names for the baby that Jacquelyn was carrying. Their home had been restored to a state of peace and love.

While watching them in my mind, Solomon stood at attention and began wagging his tail excitedly. He felt me. I needed to stop now. I channeled my meditative thoughts in another direction and focused on who I had become.

I liked it.

I liked living as Odara and for the first time I wasn't preoccupied with the idea of having a "normal" life. I was a warrior of the second sentry for the highest good of the universe. I received gifts from the Sacred Council that no one else had ever received.

I hadn't assumed full spiritual ascension yet. In laymen terms, that meant that I was an official badass.

I chanted for a few minutes to open myself up for the day and then I went inside to get my coffee. When I came back out to sit in my swing, there was a gift in the seat.

Two large feathers were fused together at the bottom. I felt the heat from the intensity of Jerod's kisses as I said thank you aloud to him. I could feel him making love to me as if we were actually in the act of doing so. I stood there holding the feathers.

I pressed them close to my heart and went inside to place them in a stone decorative box that was charged to follow me. From there, I went from room to room commanding things that I needed to prepare to move and commanded things that weren't of special use or that needed to be discarded.

After finishing the last room, I prepared to shower, dress, and get out of the house for a while.

I recalled that there was a jazz quartet that played every evening between six and seven o'clock at the local coffee shop.

I loved jazz, good wine, and warm summer nights when the moon was almost full. It was waning now, but it was good and bright, and it made me feel like the universe had my back.

I put on a simple black tank dress, high heeled sandals, and stuck a flower in my ridiculously large, radiant, living afro. Then I headed out to relax and have some fun exchanging life stories with strangers.

The music was awesome. The quartet nailed it and I was grateful for time just to be and get my spirit fed by the music.

I walked over to the piano, put a $50 tip in the jar, and I requested Miles Davis', *Some Kind of Blue.*

The piano player acknowledged me with a thumb's up and I returned to my seat with a champagne split and water.

I sat in that seat until closing while talking to a young woman who was struggling with whether she had overreacted to her boyfriend's actions earlier that day. He wouldn't answer her calls.

We laughed about the fragility of the male ego and thanked each other for the conversation.

I got home in less than five minutes, courtesy of the Uber that I called. I was pretty tipsy from the champagne and went directly into the bathroom to look at myself. "Not bad for a thousand year old woman. Not bad at all."

After stroking my own slightly inebriated ego, I got into bed and attempted to sleep. It usually took less than a half hour for me to doze off, turn over to stretch out, and stay asleep. However, after turning over, I didn't fall back to sleep.

I felt the beginning of what was definitely another episode of heat in the palms of my hands. I couldn't believe it.

I thought I would get a week but noooo... in just two days, I was already getting a call. It was a faint, heated twinge; but it was the prelude to a call, nonetheless.

I turned over and went to sleep. I knew that by the time I would awaken, the assignment that I was expecting could possibly present itself and I was ready.

The next morning, I felt fantastic. I put on one of my favorite music playlists and performed all the tracks on *Aretha Sings the Blues* dressed in my favorite lounging kimono which was paired with my hairbrush.

The latter served as my microphone. I was in full stride mid song as I sang, *Muddy Water* at the top of my lungs.

Suddenly, there was a knock at my front door. I was surprised because I only had three friends in this city and two of them had no idea where I lived.

Maybe I had ordered something and had forgotten. I went to the door expecting the FedEx man and opened it to see a beautiful woman in her late sixties.

I stared at her without being able to speak a word. She was dressed like I would be. She had the same skin, eyes and demeanor.

She greeted me, "Good Morning, Love."

At that moment I realized that she *was* me, years older. I almost fainted but caught myself with the doorsill and said, "Hello."

I wasn't sure what was happening. I knew that it wasn't trouble because—well, there was no heat in my palms and she—or whatever this was felt good.

After gathering my wits, I invited her in. She looked around and approvingly smiled at the way the house was decorated. I waited and watched.

We were in the sitting room when I said, "My apologies. Would you like some coffee or tea?"

"Yes. Coffee, please and thank you," she responded.

I finished for her, "With cream and lots of sugar and cinnamon?"

We made eye contact and she knew that I knew who she was just as well as she knew who I was.

After a few minutes in the kitchen, I brought our coffee and sat down across from her.

"*Muddy Water* is one of my favorite songs on that album," she said before taking the first sip of her coffee. I turned the music down with the remote and said nothing. I was completely fascinated seeing myself, my mannerisms, and hearing my speech pattern from an older me.

"I am here to share some things with you. I received a message that let me know my karmic debts had been paid and that I was free to live my life in peace after revealing myself," said the older Odara.

I felt my heart slow down and my mind, relax. I took a deep breath and she continued. "I am from the same realm as you. I was created to do the same work and participate in the same warfare.

"Twenty-five years ago, I assumed the form of Odara. I chose her just like you did—because she was amazing, interesting, and I liked her.

"I was given a couple of assignments that I flew through victoriously and I enjoyed living in this house being Odara in human form. Then I met someone that I was assigned to protect. I fell in love with him—deeply in love, and I began to question if I wanted the life of a spirit warrior or the life of Odara as a human being.

"He was incredible and we were inseparable. We grew closer and closer and my torment and conflict began to haunt the human in me.

"As a young warrior, I had not learned how to fully separate myself from emotion yet.

"The day came that my call required me to protect him from a spiritual attack. Instead of instinctively participating in the battle the way that I was supposed to, I revealed myself and my purpose to him, thinking it would help him understand what he needed to do to assist me.

"It did not go that way."

She paused briefly then she looked directly into my eyes.

"As you know we are never to reveal ourselves before an assignment is completed. I found out why that day. Because he loved me so much and he did not understand the magnitude of my abilities, he went in search of his enemy.

"He thought that he could get rid of him on his own and protect me from any possible harm. He was in no way shape or form prepared for or a match for what he was up against.

"As a result of this, he lost his life. When I arrived to do battle his body had expired, and the force that he had battled was gone.

"There was a saving grace, though. The spirit who took my loves life was also a young warrior and did not complete its assignment.

"He forgot to take possession of my loves spirit. I used the containment incantation and sent my love's spirit to the safety of our realm. He would remain there indefinitely until called upon again.

"When the Sacred Council appeared in my home, I knew that I was in big trouble. They informed me that my carelessness due to human emotion had had a ripple effect.

"It turned out that the man I had fallen in love with was on a direct path to make a universal difference, and I had cost him his life. Expectedly, I was stripped of all rank, power, and authority. I would be banished and live the rest of my time in the spirit realm only to watch what others were doing. I was devastated.

"Bitol, the Mayan Sky God/Creator, took pity on me and returned to the Council to suggest a reprieve. They debated while I begged for any possible opportunity to prove myself as worthy.

"It was decided that I would continue to exist in human form and age quietly and live a simple life. I was told that the Council would allow another warrior to assume Odara's body taking over at the age that I was at the time of my mistake.

"If that warrior was successful in restoring the balance that I had disrupted, I would be free from all karmic debt and allowed to regain some of my abilities to conjure and heal.

"I was also told that there was a young woman who had been chosen to carry a child that would change the perspective of humanity. The spirit of my lost love would return to this realm and have the chance to fulfill its purpose once again through her as a vessel.

"The unborn child is the brother of your beloved, Sudan. He bears the spirit of the love that I lost. The entity that you battled and defeated was the same spirit that killed him once before.

"Had it succeeded the assignment would have been carried out completely. You, young Odara, righted the balance and as a result, my debts are paid, and I am now free. I honor you."

Then she added, "I am curious, if you don't mind me asking, what is your call?"

I was so overwhelmed by what she had just shared all at once, I almost didn't answer.

"Oh, I'm sorry, my call is fire. It comes through the palms of my hands embedded with embers from my creation."

She took my hand and smiled. "I bid you well, Machaneka, now Odara. I just answered an ad for the job of live in nanny for the family that you know. I will protect them with my life and see to my love reaching his destiny.

"Your call is coming soon. I will return to this home to cleanse it after you leave and restore it to a natural habitat free from spiritual connections that won't disrupt the lives of the next people to reside here.

"It was a pleasure seeing what I would've been had I done things right the first time." She stood up and we shared a long embrace.

Both of us were in tears and silent before she left. We walked to the front door, turned towards one another and then said, "Besatah!"

I poured a glass of Branson Cognac, lit the fireplace in my bedroom, and sat on the floor. I couldn't believe what I had just heard.

That was a lot. I toasted to the sky and said, "Thank you for sending me to tell me how I became me and why everything that happened had to happen!

"Can I please get a drama free assignment where I'm filthy rich and pampered if there is such a thing?"

I heard soft laughter in the wind, and I laughed aloud. I picked up my glass to sip my French Cognac and the ice melted right in front of my eyes.

I set the glass down and looked at my hands. They were glowing with heat. I felt a strong breeze which should have been impossible since I was on the floor by the fireplace with all doors and windows closed.

Looking in the direction from which the breeze came, I saw beautiful flowers blowing in the wind in a field. The scent of fresh flowers in the morning air was hypnotic and wonderful.

I had been reassigned. The first thing I saw was the beauty of Mother Nature at her finest.

I stood taking note that my apparel appeared to be that of the affluent class during the Parisian Renaissance.

Now to start a conversation with the artist who was painting my portrait and see if I could gather any information as to what was in store for me next.

Let the knowing begin.

Contact Info

Instagram - carlajsart

Facebook - facebook.com/carlajsart

Twitter - isisthepoet

For more information including bookings and sponsorship opportunities:

www.carlajlawson.com

www.ingramcontent.com/pod-product-compliance
Lightning Source LLC
Chambersburg PA
CBHW071452080526
44587CB00014B/2077